OUR ERIC

A PORTRAIT OF ERIC PORTMAN

OUR ERIC

A PORTRAIT OF ERIC PORTMAN

Andy Owens

© Andy Owens, 2013

All Rights Reserved. No part of this publication may be reproduced, stored in a retrieval system, or transmitted in any form or by any means – electronic, mechanical, photocopying, recording, or otherwise – without prior written permission from the publisher or a licence permitting restricted copying issued by the Copyright Licensing Agency, 90 Tottenham Court Road, London W1P 0LA. This book may not be lent, resold, hired out or otherwise disposed of by trade in any form of binding or cover other than that in which it is published, without the prior consent of the publisher.

Moral Rights: The author has asserted his moral right to be identified as the Author of this Work.

Published by Sigma Leisure – an imprint of
Sigma Press, Stobart House, Pontyclerc, Penybanc Road, Ammanford, Carmarthenshire SA18 3HP.

British Library Cataloguing in Publication Data
A CIP record for this book is available from the British Library.

ISBN: 978-1-85058-981-5

Typesetting and Design by: Sigma Press, Ammanford.

Cover picture: © Max Rosher

Printed by: TJ International Ltd, Padstow, Cornwall

Disclaimer: the information in this book is given in good faith and is believed to be correct at the time of publication. No responsibility is accepted by either the author or publisher for errors or omissions, or for any loss or injury howsoever caused.

CONTENTS

Preface — 7
Foreword by Professor Andrew Spicer — 8
Foreword by Michael and John Portman — 10
Introduction — 11

Chapter 1 – Made To Measure — 17
Chapter 2 – Stage and Screen — 33
Chapter 3 – Life Begins at Forty — 55
Chapter 4 – Pals at Penpol — 89
Chapter 5 – Acting Up — 99
Chapter 6 – The Rattigan Connection — 113
Chapter 7 – Choose A Part For Portman — 139
Chapter 8 – Never A Night So Grand — 145
Chapter 9 – A Tipple Too Far — 167
Chapter 10 – The Final Curtain — 177

Appendix – Films/TV/Radio — 195
Appendix – Stage Plays — 207

Bibliography/Sources — 217
Acknowledgements — 218
Index — 222

For Eric Portman's nephews and cousins: John Portman, Michael Portman, Anne Womersley and Patricia Duggan for all their help – and without whom this book would have been impossible.

PREFACE

'Eric Portman was a very big presence. He was a great actor, no doubt about it. I had seen him in a lot of films and he was incredible, the way he did everything. He was a very polished actor who never overshot the mark. He had that wonderful voice. There was something about his tone that was a Yorkshire thing. It was such a marvellous voice and he was such a realistic person. He was what he believed he was and he was perfect doing it. He was a marvellous man, and very kind to me. He used to say: "Oh, he'll be alright. He's way ahead of us," meaning me, but of course it was he who was way ahead of me.'

'There was no fuss about Eric; he just did it. He was just an ordinary person doing an ordinary job of work, except that he happened to be a terrific actor, a great performer and a great personality. He was with the greats, definitely, and it was a pity he didn't get a knighthood. He was very undersold – he should have had that sort of accolade.'

The actor Richard Briers, CBE (1934-2013)
as told to journalist and author Tony Earnshaw tonyearnshaw.com

FOREWORD
BY PROFESSOR ANDREW SPICER

Eric Portman was one of the leading British male actors of the 1940s, second only to James Mason in popularity – as shown by readers' polls in *Picturegoer* – and with a greater dramatic range. His extensive work in theatre and television has not been preserved, but we have his film performances many of which leave a lasting impression. The one that instantly springs to mind is his 'breakthrough' role as Lieutenant Hurth in the wartime melodrama *The 49th Parallel*, the first of three films he made with Michael Powell and Emeric Pressburger. Portman deliberately avoided the easy stereotype of the automaton Nazi braggart by playing his character sympathetically, thereby producing a chilling and compelling depiction of a man in thrall to a corrupt ideology in which he sincerely believes. After the war, Portman specialised in the tortured portrayal of murderers and criminals in a series of films – *Daybreak, The Mark of Cain, Corridor of Mirrors, Wanted For Murder* and *Dear Murderer* – that, paradoxically, endeared him to the British public through their compassionate renderings of men afflicted by personal and social trauma. One could see these films as part of a wider group, which would include the wonderful *Great Day*, in which Portman plays the 'damaged man', someone of strong character and great potential who has been psychologically affected by the war.

However, that grouping would only encompass one strand of Portman's range as an actor. He could play high-ranking figures – one thinks here of his marvellously subtle portrait of the Senior British Officer, Colonel Richmond, in *The Colditz Story* – and ordinary men – his blunt northern works foreman in *Millions Like Us*. Towards the latter stages of his career he played down-and-outs and misfits, as in Michael Winner's underrated *West 11*, and in Bryan Forbes' *The Whisperers* in which he gives perhaps his finest performance, a masterpiece of manipulative callousness. Portman was prepared to take great risks as an actor, never striving to become the bland, ubiquitous leading man and carefully avoiding being tied to a long-term studio contract with either the Rank Organisation or the Associated British Pictures Corporation. He valued being able to choose his own roles and to move between film, theatre and television, respecting each as a particular medium in which he could refine his craft as an actor.

When I first wrote about Eric Portman for the book *Typical Men*, I was surprised and frustrated about how little had been written about Portman and baffled that an actor I thought so powerful and compelling had become forgotten. At long last, a biography has appeared. Andy Owens takes us through Portman's somewhat chequered career and his diligent research has uncovered much new or forgotten material. He has pulled together the lineaments of a fascinating life rooted in Halifax, the Yorkshire town in which Portman was born. In doing so, he has rectified confusions and clarified facts – date and place of birth – and has provided a fascinating and wide-ranging portrait drawn from the views and opinions of a broad conspectus of people, many of whom knew Portman personally. I hope that this book will help rescue this prodigiously gifted actor from his current obscurity and foster the interest and appreciation in Portman that his talents fully deserve.

Professor Andrew Spicer
University of the West of England, Bristol
March 2013

FOREWORD
BY MICHAEL AND JOHN PORTMAN

As Halifax-born nephews of Eric Portman, who remember him at the height of his fame in the 1940s and '50s, we were approached by Andy Owens, a Halifax author, who wanted to write about him.

To the surprise of Mr Owens, and many other people, there did not exist a biography of one of Britain's most famous film stars and most successful stage actors in London and on Broadway.

We were impressed with Andy's attitude and writing, and his genuine interest in conducting detailed research with family, and with newspapers, and film and theatre archives. It has opened our eyes to the many interesting aspects of Eric Portman's life and career for which we thank the author.

Michael and John Portman

INTRODUCTION

Eric Portman (1901-1969) appeared in over forty films, numerous stage plays and many TV productions, on either side of the Atlantic. He was born in the same town as me – Halifax, West Yorkshire – and was affectionately known by local people as 'Our Eric', hence the title of the book.

He famously walked out on a Hollywood contract with Warner Brothers after being under-used, playing the character 'First Lord' in Errol Flynn movie *The Prince and the Pauper*. And yet four years later, he achieved international stardom playing the sadistic Nazi U-Boat commander, Lieutenant Hurth, in the Powell-and-Pressburger film *The 49th Parallel*. He went on to star in two more of their movies: *One Of Our Aircraft is Missing* and *A Canterbury Tale*.

As an actor, he had an extremely wide-range and took on many different character types, ranging from authority figures and bluff northerners to seedy criminals and damaged men.

He co-starred with John Mills in *The Colditz Story* and *We Dive at Dawn*, and his final major role was in the film *Deadfall*, directed by Bryan Forbes, and playing opposite Michael Caine.

Eric saw his first play in 1908, at the age of seven, at the Grand Theatre, Halifax. And in 1956, when the Grand was threatened with closure, he brought the entire West End cast and crew of Terence Rattigan's play *Separate Tables* to Halifax, to attract new audiences and save the theatre from closure. The company worked without pay, on their day off work, and did a 400-mile round trip from London to Halifax. The set was copied in exact detail, and the whole cast stayed in a Leeds hotel – all at Eric Portman's expense. This was the first – and, as far as I know, the only – time any such project had been attempted. The book has a whole chapter dedicated to this episode, including much local press coverage and a letter I received from the former manager of the theatre.

Although he developed a drinking problem later in life, and had a few tiffs with two of his leading ladies, Eric's kind and generous nature were widely acknowledged. He helped many charities, and also donated the profits of his fan club to the RSPCA.

There are two possible reasons why Eric is not as well remembered as fellow leading actors of his generation such as Laurence Olivier, Ralph Richardson or John Gielgud.

Firstly, there has never been a previous book about him. He had a very private life and none of his friends or relatives would ever betray him to the press. In fact, he was so guarded that when the famous theatre critic Kenneth Tynan approached Eric with the idea of writing his biography, he was angrily rebuffed.

Another possible reason is because many of his films were never previously shown on TV, or released on video. However, with the recent release of some of his classic movies on DVD, with others regularly broadcast on TV, and many excerpts from his films available on YouTube, interest in his life and work has increased, even amongst younger generations – evident from the comments on a variety of movie websites – and yet still no biography has appeared.

I get the impression that people are constantly trying to produce biographies of Eric Portman. In fact, when I contacted Bryan Forbes, CBE, who directed Eric in two films, he replied: 'Just this morning, by a strange coincidence, I have also replied to another Portman biographer!' In fact, various people who contacted me during my research, wrote: 'I hope you succeed where many others have failed.'

But why *have* other budding biographers failed? From my own experience, there is not much printed information about Eric. Lists of his films, TV and stage appearances are included on various websites, together with archives of interviews available in back issues of newspapers and magazines. Yet this alone is not sufficient material to provide a writer with enough text to fill a book which most publishers would demand for a biography.

The two advantages I had were: 1) I was born in the same town as Eric Portman and therefore have had access to archives in the local newspaper, *Halifax Courier*, and the Editor and staff were kind enough to invite me to hunt through their files, and I found more material in Calderdale Libraries and from Halifax Civic Trust; 2) I made a media appeal for information – via emails sent to two hundred newspapers, magazines and websites in the UK – asking for their readers to contact me if they could help with my research, which is a method I used for researching some of my previous books.

These combined sources have allowed me to access and present a much broader picture of the actor than was previously available. Many editors and journalists took an interest in promoting my research, not to mention around fifty kind souls who replied to my appeal – nephews, cousins, friends, friends-of-friends, colleagues, neighbours, acquaintances, fans – together with invaluable assistance I received from many librarians, archivists, historians, website owners and countless others – each of them enabling me to add very worthwhile pieces to the jigsaw that was Eric Portman's life.

While some of the memories are just a few sentences long – people who knew the actor very briefly – even these provide insightful and fascinating snapshots into the actor's life, both on-and-off the screen.

Among those who replied to my appeal were his nephews, John and Michael Portman who, like me, were also busy researching their Uncle's life – not for a book – but for the sake of gathering memories for their children and grandchildren. They also took the time to travel up to Halifax to meet me, to help fill the gaps in my research, and so I could pass on to them anything new I had learned about their uncle. I received some truly unique photographs from two of Eric's cousins: Anne Womersley and Patricia Duggan. Not to mention numerous others who sent me little-known press cuttings, magazine interviews and autographed photos. Without the help of these kind people, this book would simply not exist.

And this has certainly been the most satisfying part of the research: the privilege of receiving first-hand accounts – personal memories – of people who had some connection with Eric Portman, together with never-before-published photographs and other documents such as private family letters, with people entrusting me with the task of recording them for posterity, preserving those memories and archives for future generations.

If any readers are expecting a shocking exposé, full of scandal and controversy, they are going to be sadly disappointed. Despite being gay, at a ridiculous time when it was illegal to be so, Eric managed to largely avoid the homophobic spite of gossip columnists and hacks.

If I have made any mistakes, or omitted to mention any part of Mr Portman's life, however trivial it may seem, please could you send me details, c/o my website or publisher's address, as I will be grateful to receive them and happy to incorporate these in a possible future edition of this book.

Eric Portman, forever modest, claimed that much of his success was down to good luck. But the fact is most of his success was down to sheer hard work, commitment and a passion for the stage, which then translated very well to film, radio and TV, when opportunities in those emerging mediums presented themselves. He was also known for his kindness and generosity and an 'un-affected' manner in his celebrity status, and he always felt very privileged to find himself getting well paid for doing a job he loved. More than anything else, these factors must surely account for his successes in life, both personally and professionally, and I hope I have done him justice.

Thank you very much for reading this book.

Andy Owens
www.andyowenbooks.co.uk
Halifax, March 2013

CHAPTER 1

MADE TO MEASURE

Many things occurred on 13th July 1901.

It was reported that the Board of Trade told the Tramways Committee that people could spit *from* trams, though not *in* or *on* them, and a newspaper commented: 'This will go a long way towards removing the objections of those gentlemen who expectorate, but pedestrians will still have to be watchful when passing a car.'

On the same day, a deaf and dumb couple were married by an ordained priest who was similarly afflicted, and Raffaelo Virgilio, a 'cripple' from Italy, was arrested in Blackpool for 'obstructing a footpath by playing an accordion'. He was charged £5 for such a heinous crime, but as he had collected over £17 that day, I don't expect he lost much sleep over it.

On a trip to Scarborough, businessman George Thomas Fleming, from Halifax, West Yorkshire, 'complained of illness and suddenly expired,' while fellow Halifax resident A. D. Oates won first prize with his yearling filley in a stud contest in Driffield.

And on the same date in a corner of Halifax called Boothtown, in an even smaller corner of Boothtown called Ackroydon, at 71 Chester Road to be precise, Eric Harold Portman was born.

There has been some confusion over the date and place of Eric's birth, culminating in erroneous reporting in some books and other sources. In 1997, the Halifax Civic Trust erected a blue plaque outside number 20 Chester Road, proclaiming it to be Eric Portman's birthplace. But in 2009, Halifax historian and genealogist David Glover uncovered a few errors, and his findings were reported in the local newspaper.

He told the *Halifax Courier* that his copy of Eric's birth certificate sets straight some often repeated errors, namely that Eric was born at 20 Chester Road in 1903 and that his middle name was Harrison. Mr Glover found that Eric was born at 71 Chester Road in 1901, and that his middle name was Harold. Harrison was his mother's maiden name, and Mr Glover suggests that he may have sometimes used that as his middle name, perhaps as a sort of tribute to her memory. He also suggested that Eric may have discreetly knocked a couple of years off his age at one point, and then the mistake kept getting repeated!

However, there is another possible reason for two of the discrepancies. When the Editor of the *Halifax Courier* kindly invited me to the newspaper offices to scramble through the mass of press cuttings about the actor, I found a hand-written note, which read:

ERIC PORTMAN
1: Film star
Was born in
20 Chester Road,
Boothtown, HX
July 13, 1903

Underneath were some scribbled words, which read: 'from his late father.' So maybe Eric's father got the details wrong in his later years, which were passed to the media, then dutifully re-hashed by other sources.

Although Eric was born in Halifax, his father Matthew came from a coal-mining family in South Yorkshire and was the son of James Portman and Harriet Satterfit, of Thorpe Hesley, a village near Rotherham. By today's standards, it was a huge family and Matthew's siblings were Sarah, Henry, Bernard, Willie, Albert, John Edward, George E., Ada M., and the brilliantly named Friend Portman.

Although it looked as if Matthew would follow in his father's footsteps and work down the pit, he managed to escape that and become a clothes salesman. He worked as manager of a hat shop in Thorpe Hesley, belonging to a Mrs Tomlinson, and later in a similar shop at Bridgegate, Rotherham. Some years later, he was appointed manager at Hepworth's gentleman's outfitters in Burnley, where he lived in lodgings.

Matthew married Alice Harrison in 1893 and the couple moved to Halifax, where he had recently been appointed manager of *that* town's branch of Hepworths. Once settled there, the couple started a family and had four children – Charles Clifford (born in 1895), Winifred May (1897), Eric Harold (1901) and Frank Leslie (1903).

Matthew soon left Hepworth's and set up his own business as a gentlemen's outfitter, originally located in the top section of the Arcade Royal on the corner of Commercial Street and King Edward Street – the space now occupied by the Duke of Wellington public house. They also became members of All Souls' Church, in Halifax, and were both active church workers, with Matthew serving as Churchwarden for some time.

The earliest advertisement I could find for the family business was printed in the *Halifax Daily Guardian* on Tuesday 1st January 1918, which read:

MATTHEW PORTMAN FOR
Boys' Youths' and Mans' Overcoats

>   Raincoats'   Boys' Velvet Suits
>   Boys' Fancy Jerseys   Fancy Hose
>   Sports Suits   Pyjama Suits
>   Shirts Collars Ties
>   ALL USEFUL PRESENTS
>   18, ARCADE ROYAL
>   18, KING EDWARD STREET, HALIFAX

Some years later, the Co-Op bought the Arcade Royal and so Matthew moved his business to premises on Silver Street, some two hundred yards away.

In 1907, Eric's parents took him to the Grand Theatre, Halifax, to see his first play – a melodrama called *A London Actress*. Many years later, the actor would recall how his passion began. 'I was thrilled,' wrote Eric. 'I remember so well walking home that night up Haley Hill, (towards Boothtown) determined to be an actor.'

Less than a year later, the seven year old took to the stage himself, playing the role of 'Mischief' in a school production of *Bo-Peep*. A photo was taken of Eric and two little girls in the play, which was made into a postcard, presumably by his parents, and no doubt sent out as a memento to family and friends.

Eric Moorcroft, a friend of Matthew, and himself a gentleman's outfitter with a shop on Harrison Road in Halifax, recalled how the boy: '…commenced in school plays…only small parts, but his school reports stated "this boy has talent." In a year or so he was playing leads; his genius was apparent.'

This was at Trinity School in Halifax and, in later years, during one of his trips back home, Eric Portman would help the school with charity fundraising.

Eric – and no doubt his brothers Cliff and Leslie – were trained in the family business from an early age, as it was naturally expected that sons would follow their fathers' trades. After my media appeal, I received an email from Ian

Eric and friends in school play *Bo-Peep* in 1908

Portman, who told me: 'My father Ernest was a distant cousin of Eric and I remember him telling me about the time he travelled to Halifax because his Uncle Matthew…was a tailor and was going to make him his first pair of long trousers. Eric was only a young boy then, but he measured my father for his first suit.'

In 1912, Eric attended Rishworth Boarding School, whose motto was: *Res Non Verba* (Deeds Not Words), and Eric Moorcroft later recalled: 'How well I remember him as a young boy at Rishworth Grammar School, always the clean, tidy boy, just clever enough at his lessons to get by, and artistic. I still have some excellent watercolours painted by him when he was only 12.'

Margaret Medawar tells me: 'I have always taken an interest in Eric Portman since my late father who was from Halifax, told me that his brother Sammy O'Hare was in the same class at school with Eric Portman. I do remember my father saying that the young Eric always seemed a bit aloof from the other boys and was from quite a well-off family.'

If Eric was aloof, or snobbish in any way as a child, then he certainly lost it in later years. It could be said that making his own success, was the making of him.

His boyhood was spent among the bracing moors of the West Riding, and one of his hobbies, which continued throughout his life, was country walking. One journalist would later write that Eric was an amateur swimming champion, presumably while still at school and, in later years, the actor would attribute his fitness to this upbringing. 'The business of being a film actor makes tremendous demands on one, both physically and mentally,' he said. 'I often feel that without the wonderful start I had in my early environment, I should not have the vitality I have today.'

After his first year at Rishworth Boarding School, Eric suffered what Moorcroft considered to be his '...greatest loss, his beloved mother whom he loved and worshipped, died suddenly.'

A month after her 45th birthday, Alice Portman attended a service at

Eric's mother Alice Portman

All Souls Church on Sunday 9th May 1915 when, according to a local report, she '...had a seizure and was subsequently operated upon for appendicitis.' Alice was bedridden for two weeks, but '...despite every care and most skilled treatment, she passed away.'

Eric's interest in acting was not confined to school plays, as Margaret Jenkinson recounted to me when replying to my media appeal. She wrote: 'My late stepfather was Morris Dewhirst, who lived in Boothtown, not far from the Portman family. 'Dad' often used to tell me that when he and my Uncle Cyril were in their teens, Eric was a friend of theirs and every Saturday evening they would act in small plays or make up a show at Grandmother's house and invite the neighbours in. Grandmother would hang her clothes-line across the room and drape over a large curtain, and their impromptu show would begin. Seemingly, the neighbours loved it all and it was somewhere to go on the dark winter nights.'

Many years later, Miss Nellie Gee wrote to the *Halifax Courier* recalling these early attempts at drama: "(Eric) produced a play to be acted in the living room of his home and my brother had a part in it. Unfortunately, I cannot remember the name of the play, but we went after school and the price of the ticket for the evening performance was two pins! It was all most enjoyable." (© Halifax Courier Ltd)

After school, Eric still had a strong interest in drama which just wouldn't let go. He helped form a concert party, the Aristocrats, at All Souls' Church, Boothtown, whose members included his sister Winifred and the daughters of locally renowned musician Shackleton Pollard – who lived next door to the Portmans. Eric was also a driving force behind other productions, and Halifax resident C.E.D. Bottomley recalled many years later, how Eric '...ran a small show, along with Mr L. Locke and his two daughters and an orchestra of which I was the leader. The show was staged for the At Homes

Eric and friends in concert party *The Aristocrats*. Note Eric's sister Winifred, on the extreme left in each photograph

concert at All Souls for many years.' Eric also spent time with theatre groups of the Halifax YMCA, King Cross Amateur Dramatic Society and the Halifax Light Opera Society.

Many years later, the journalist John Y. Stapelton observed that: '…his speaking voice has a thrilling quality which has never, to my knowledge, been successfully imitated by radio impersonators.'

And there may be a very good reason for that.

During his time in the HLOS, in 1921, Eric appeared in the show *Tom Jones*, and had quite a close friendship with other cast members including Shirley Robertshaw's parents. Ms Robertshaw told me: 'Eric played the role of Squire Weston in the show. He actually lost his voice as he had to shout so much. It never came back properly and this was why he had a hoarse-type of voice.'

But despite Eric's love for all things theatrical, he still had to earn a living and it seemed he was destined to succeed his father in the family business as a gentleman's outfitter.

Eric Moorcroft recalled how '…it was his father's wish to come into the family business and being a considerate son, he acceded to this request, but his heart was in the stage, not gentleman's outfitting.'

The book *Between You and Me*, is the autobiography of fellow Halifax-born actor and broadcaster Wilfred Pickles (1904-1978), who had been a member of the King Cross Amateur Dramatic Society with Eric, and Pickles wrote of their friendship.

Eric visits former cast members of the Halifax Light Opera Society's production of *Tom Jones* (Courtesy of the Halifax Light Opera Society)

While Eric's father was a gentlemen's outfitter, Wilfred's father was a builder, and yet neither young actor wanted to follow in their respective family trades.

Wilfred described Eric as a '…young, embryo actor (who) started his stage career in Halifax at the same time. He was a handsome lad with an unusual personality. I knew him well because he had been to school at Rishworth with my brother Arthur; our mutual interest in the theatre brought us together, and I used to slip into his father's shop where we would talk about acting and plays and actors and playwrights for hours on end. We would be discussing the possibilities of *Hamlet* or *Twelfth Night* when a customer would enter. My friend would contort his face into an expression of frustration and rebellion, continue the discussion for a moment or two longer and then break off to serve a tie or shirt. He hated it all just as I hated building. Such was the early single-mindedness of Eric Portman.'

However, between working as a builder and becoming a professional actor, Wilfred Pickles also worked for a gentleman's outfitter in Halifax, so Eric's early career seems to have rubbed off on his friend!

On 18th March 1918, while Eric was working in his father's shop, he sent a letter to his younger brother Leslie who was a pupil at Rishworth Boarding School. It refers to an army tank being on display to the public in Halifax. This was a fundraising effort to attract the crowds and raise money for the war effort, to help the government with the costs of providing the army with more tanks and armoury. The notepaper of the letter was headed: *M. Portman's – Gentleman's Outfitter*. The letter read:

My Dear Les,

Dad has asked me to write and tell you that he is sorry he has forgotten to get you the PO (you want one shilling for a brush, don't you?) but that he will send you 1/6 tomorrow.

You see, we have been so busy, with the tank being here as there are hundreds of strangers visiting the town, bigger than the one we saw at Bradford, I think, and it is the one that has been in action. There is a big hole up-front where it has been shot at, and several other 'wounds'. It wasn't opened until 12.30pm today and up to now they have got £630,000, (*donated by businesses, organisations and individuals), I think it is very good, don't you? Of course, there is the usual crowd of men selling tank brooches,

Eric's letter to his brother Leslie on notepaper from his father's shop – dated 1918

photographs, etc, and you can hardly move in George Square. I wish you could get over to see it. All the schoolchildren went this morning. They have had the day off. Mr Pickard invested £1000 for the schools. I suppose you will be having the 'camouflaged' tank at Rishworth. It is a very good imitation, but rather too nice, I think. I think I shall come up on Easter Monday and you will soon be home now. Our 'Darling' (*family dog) is getting a right wild one. He grunts/growls something awful. Winnie told you how I found him in Wheater's (*a local pub) didn't she? I've lost him for two nights last week. The third night I found him sleeping on Cliff's empty bed.

Well, I haven't time for any more now, so I shall have to stop.

    Best love from everybody,

    Your loving brother,

        Eric.

Eric Moorcroft, who would later become involved in the management of the Grand Theatre, Halifax, where Eric had seen his first play, wrote how young Eric's early roles in amateur stage productions: '…did not please his father, as the Saturday afternoon matinees meant (he) was leaving father to cope with a busy shop, so you will understand what arguments went on between them.'

Perhaps this is the reason why Eric spent some time working as a salesman for Marshall and Snelgrove's Department Store in Leeds. But his father needn't have worried about the future of the family business, for Eric's younger brother Leslie would take over from him at the shop.

The journalist John Stapelton later wrote: 'I feel that had (Eric) stuck to his early job as a salesman in a Leeds Department Store, he would today be a leading figure in the commercial world, but that the world of art would have suffered a grievous loss.'

Eric Portman was the biggest film star Halifax ever produced.. In this publicity picture from the late 1950s he is seen serving a customer, his nephew John Portman, in the shop his father kept in the old Arcade Royale. Can any readers remember the shop?

Eric revisits his father's shop and serves his nephew John Portman
(Courtesy of the Halifax Courier Ltd)

When the actor Henry Baynton brought his theatre group – Robert Courtneidge's Shakespeare Company – to Halifax to perform *Julius Caesar* at the town's Theatre Royal, Baynton managed to astound everybody, by packing the audience from floor to ceiling, and 'house full' notices had to be posted outside.

Eighteen year old Eric went to see the show. Afterwards, he went backstage to see Baynton and secured a job with the company.

Many years later in 1948, journalist John Ware interviewed Eric, asking: 'How do you turn from shop assistant into a famous actor?' Eric replied: 'There is no recipe for this secret any more than there is for becoming a great writer, painter or musician, except the common ingredient of hard work and some luck. But mostly hard work. I went on the stage because I knew somebody in a touring Shakespearean company. My mother had died when I was thirteen. My father, not knowing quite what to do with me, didn't seriously object.'

'I never experienced the early struggles most actors seem to have suffered. Or, perhaps I did, but so enjoyed them that they have left me without regrets. I decided when I was at Rishworth School, on the Yorkshire Moors, that I was going to be an actor. It never occurred to me to safeguard against a precarious livelihood by training myself for acting or by taking up a sideline. I could have done so, I suppose. I could have worked in my father's office (and shop) while I studied at a dramatic school. I did neither. I learnt the acting thing by joining a touring company, playing parts and learning by my mistakes. Thank goodness I didn't have to go to a drama school – tiresome things. In the Shakespearean Repertory Company I didn't earn much – about £2 a week – but it was enough to live on.'

He was given a job on the understanding that he was to be a sort of dresser-cum-secretary to the leading actor, Henry Baynton himself, who was appearing at the Opera House in Manchester.

'Naturally,' said Eric, 'I decided to play Romeo as soon as possible.'

But he was prepared to do any acting work at all, and within a few months, he made his first stage appearance in a small part in *Richard II* staged at the Victoria Hall, Sunderland, in 1924.

When Baynton's company returned to Halifax, it saw Eric playing the title role in a play called *Don*. *The Halifax Guardian* reported that:

'Mr Eric Portman, taking the part of Don, played in his home town for the first time in his professional career. It seems but yesterday that he appeared in the Theatre Royal, as an amateur with the Light Opera Society, in *Tom Jones*. Six years, however, lie between then and now, and in that space, Mr Portman has made rapid strides. He left Halifax, and is now an actor who commands an enthusiastic notice of the critics wherever he plays.'

'But Mr Portman showed last night that he is not merely a Shakespearean actor. Indeed, he surprised Halifax with the playing of Don. It was a performance which justified the opinion of Mr Baynton, expressed in February of this year: "I can assure you that Portman is going to make a name for himself." Mr Baynton's forecast will certainly be fulfilled. It is inevitable if Eric Portman – of Halifax, remember – can sustain the ability that he displayed at the Theatre Royal last night.'

'It is not often that a Halifax audience lingers when the curtain has been rung down on a performance, but on this occasion it did, and having applauded the company with unusual warmth, called for Mr Portman and gave him a remarkable ovation. The hero of the evening responded in a brief and brave speech and, on retiring, must have felt that he had not let himself down in his native town. It may be said, indeed, that if we could have more plays of the arresting quality of *Don*, and more actors of the calibre of Mr Portman, Mr Baynton's repertory season would be an amazing success. There was a large house, which will certainly be maintained throughout the week.' (© Halifax Courier Ltd)

In his autobiography, Wilfred Pickles further recalled how Eric's name was now displayed on posters outside the theatre, advertising the show. He wrote:

'My brother Arthur and I decided to telephone him and ask him to have tea with us and talk over old times. We arranged a meeting in the town. As Arthur and I waited for him, we talked about Eric and his acting and

Eric returns to Halifax to perform at the Theatre Royal (Courtesy of the Halifax Courier Ltd)

exchanged theories about what improvement he might have made under Baynton.'

'I noticed a figure coming towards us wearing a wide-brimmed Homburg hat pulled well down over the forehead, and a heavy gorilla-shouldered overcoat. As the man drew close, I joked loudly to Arthur: 'Here he is!"

'We both laughed.'

'But it was indeed Eric! He was now the complete actor and, just as I had once walked down the queue in the half-light hoping they would take me for an actor, Eric, I thought, was now carrying off a development of that form of exhibitionism, pretending to himself that he was a stranger playing in a strange land. He even asked us the way to St James's Road, one of the main streets of Halifax. But Eric, whose voice then, was just as it is known now to millions of moviegoers, was a very fine actor. I find him consistently amusing and grand company. To me, Eric was the man with the torch. He had started out and, in doing so, had shown me the way.'

Wilfred Pickles would go on to be a radio personality and later a character actor in several films, most notably playing Geoffrey Fisher in John Schlesinger's version of Keith Waterhouse's classic comedy *Billy Liar* (1963), starring Tom Courtenay in the title role. This is one of several films in which Pickles would play a Yorkshireman and, although Eric would play a few Yorkshiremen himself, he was evidently not content to specialise in portraying just one type. His aim was to play as many different types of characters as he could. Not only out of a passion for acting, but also to aim for versatility and to avoid being pigeon-holed.

As Eric wrote years later in an essay on acting: 'If you have only a little talent, and a lot of personality, you may succeed – as a type. This means you will always be cast for the same parts. Your film life will, then, not be a long one… shorter than you might wish it to be. In fact, the public will probably tire of you before the studio executives. The public has to be impressed by real acting before it will grant stars long life on the screen. Otherwise the favourite game is to make and break. It is the old business…of killing the god. The blood heritage of a myth, of enormous psychological importance, urges cinemagoers to say, "Oh, my dear, he's absolutely finished. Of course, they never do last long, do they?" And this of their favourite of yesterday. The ritual slaying of the star is compensation, a way of working out jealousy. It's only the star with acting ability who need not fear the sinister side of his admirers.'

While Wilfred Pickles certainly *did* have a lot of talent, the career path he chose was as a performer, based mainly on his voice and personality, and he went on to be a very successful and much-loved presenter of radio programmes – together with his wife Mabel – rather than a dramatic actor like his friend Eric.

CHAPTER 2

STAGE AND SCREEN

Although Eric had his name on posters outside theatres advertising the plays, he would later recall his life off the stage. He said he would never forget the succeeding procession of theatrical digs 'on those Sundays on which it always rains', when his landlady would turn him out because she wanted the house to herself for an hour or two!

His first stage role in London was 'Antipholus of Syracruse' in William Shakespeare's *The Comedy of Errors* performed at the Savoy in 1924, and although there is no record of how long the play ran, he had to wait a year for his next major role, playing 'Mowbray' in another Shakespeare play *Richard II* at the Strand.

Eric spent three years touring in provincial stock companies, sometimes playing modern repertory, sometimes in classic drama. But he first went to London at the age of 23, appearing in three West End flops. He later described them as 'sensational failures' because each play was written by a famous author and should have been a success. They were *The Roof* by John Galsworthy, *Sheppey* by W. Somerset Maugham, and *On the Rocks* by George Bernard Shaw. Although the plays failed, Eric's performances earned him the reputation of being a reliable and intelligent actor.

'The result of these minor achievements was a succession of juvenile leads,' he later told a journalist. 'It wasn't for years that I made a real hit. For me, life began at 40.'

A press report stated that:
"Mr Eric Portman, the Halifax actor, has had the distinction of appearing in the first production of Galsworthy's play *The Roof* at the Vaudeville Theatre, London. He takes the part of 'A Young Man', described as 'a polo-playing poet.' "It is a delightful part", he writes, and declares his fervent appreciation of a love scene which he shares with Madeleine Carrol in the role of 'A Young Woman.' This is in Scene 5, devoted entirely to a delightfully humorous bedroom dialogue. In the middle of the scene, Mr Portman has to recite a forty-four poetic avowel of love. People who have read *The Roof* will realise that he has quite a prominent part to play, and, according to accounts, he is playing it very well."

Eric Portman and Madeleine Carroll as A Young Man and A Young Woman.

Eric Portman, Madeleine Carroll and cast of John Galsworthy's stage play *The Roof* (source unknown)

In 1926, he played a small role in the play *White Cargo*, and the next January he did a three-month repertory tour of modern plays. That April, he was back at the Old Vic playing 'classic' texts, such as Orestes in *Electra of Euripdes* and Horatio in *Hamlet*.

He spent another four months in London, at the Lyric Theatre, Hammersmith, performing in the repertory season, playing Lucentio in *The Taming of the Shrew*, Bassanio in *Henry V*, and Claudio in *Much Ado About Nothing*.

Alan Sidney-Wilmot told me how the cast of a repertory theatre club would have approached their work. He said: 'The cast would be performing in one play in the evenings, while in the daytime they were learning the lines for the next play – the performance of which would be performed as soon as the first had completed its run, and at the same time, they would be reading parts for the play after that.' This must have culminated in a gruelling schedule but would have proven invaluable experience for the cast.

Although Eric never spoke specifically of his experience in repertory, I was eager to learn more of this form of theatre, so we can better understand his early working life as an actor. I found copies of the short-lived *Repertory* magazine, which ran for just ten weekly issues between 2nd January 1950 and 6th March 1950, with articles written by people who would, in later years, not only become film stars in their own right, but also Eric's co-stars. The writers of the articles were Dennis Price who would appear with Eric in *A Canterbury Tale* and *Dear Murderer* and Flora Robson who co-starred with him in *Great Day*.

Flora Robson wrote:
'To work in repertory for a few years is to serve an apprenticeship in the theatre. Alas! Too many young people nowadays will not do the hard work

necessary for such intensive study and training. To learn any craft thoroughly, or to study for a profession, there are years of concentrated effort for very little remuneration. Yet these years do pay – they pay in very vital experience. That is why I am so convinced that repertory is a grand training ground for those who mean to act. The years in repertory may be hard and lean, but the experience gained is worth some sacrifices, worth some disappointments. There are disappointments. Learning a new play each week, the actor succeeds in getting a broad outline of his part and the play as a whole. There is little chance of intense detailed work until perhaps the last two nights of the play, then some of these details begin to appear. Unfortunately, the brief run is nearly over. Yet for all that, the fact remains that sometimes there is a spark in a repertory production which does not appear in a more elaborate presentation of the same play. We know how hard on one, weekly repertory can be.... I have heard criticisms that repertory actors are not interested in any play in which they do not have a big part. Well, there are bad actors and good ones. Those who feel that their part is not important enough should remember that we have actors such as Gielgud, Donat and Olivier who are *real* actors, who have played and can still play with all their might, old and young parts, comedy, tragedy, and character. That is why they are at the top of our profession.'

Dennis Price wrote:
'It was just after I'd had the great luck to be in John Gielgud's famous Queen's Theatre season of four plays in 1937 – doing bits and pieces, my first join after eighteen months' Embassy Theatre training – that I applied to Tyrone Guthrie at the Old Vic for various parts he was casting. I was positively hurt and disgusted when he told me to go in repertory for at least two years and leave the idea of fat parts in long West End runs to the people

who had learned how to play them.…I don't think I have yet begun to know my job, but I'm quite certain those months spent in repertory at Croydon, Windsor, Oxford and Hull were never, for one minute, a mistake. Discipline … has gone out of the theatre, some old bores often lament. They should work in some of the repertories which, if they're any good at all, regard discipline as a strong foundation stone, in exactly the same way as do the ballet companies of any significance. Team spirit – seems to me a fundamental feature in the make-up of the theatre, the straight theatre at any rate. A repertory company should not be able to exist without it.'

'Above all, repertory teaches you that this business of being the faithful servant of the public is a twenty-four hour job. That is what life in the film world incessantly demands. Out of the twenty-four hours, just about eight are your own, and these are spent asleep. There is no minute of the rest of the day when you are not on call. The actual filming, the stills session, the personal appearances, the business of keeping fit (so tremendously important) and a dozen other chores the moguls expect from their pound of flesh. I remember in repertory, only just having enough time to eat and sleep. That was good training to enable one to face the rigours of the studio in consequence. The habit of theatre-going will never die out, come slump, come revolution or what have you.…The Comradeship, the healthy ambition and competition, the satisfaction of having played the butler one week as well as you played the duke the week before, the thrill of once in a while getting a play never before performed, and above all, the certain knowledge that *one* day, *however* long it may take, *if* you know the job *and* have the talent, opportunity will come your way. Yes, I think repertory is well-loaded with rare gifts – and I'm certain that the theatre, the films, and now television, could never exist without the people who are brought up in repertory.'

Eric continued performing with the Old Vic Theatre Company, from February to May 1928, during which time he and the actress Jean Forbes-Robertson would play the title characters in *Romeo and Juliet* performed at the Old Vic Theatre, under the direction of the famous Lilian Baylis. Eric would later recall her three-word description of him: 'Frivolous – but useful!' In one press report, Eric was described as 'the best Romeo who had been heard for years.'

In later years, Eric would comment on the actresses he played opposite on the stage, describing: 'Madeleine Carroll the most beautiful, Edith Evans the most clever, Diana Wynyard the most poised and complete, Fay Compton the most adorable, and Jean Forbes-Robertson the most neglected.'

While still only twenty-seven, Eric's name was appearing in lights outside the theatres. He played a wide range of roles in a wide range of plays, from Charles Surface in Sheridan's comedy *A School for Scandal* to Laertes in *Hamlet*. He portrayed Erhard Borkman in Henrik Ibsen's drama *John Gabriel Borkman*, and his performance as Stephen Undershaft in George Bernard Shaw's play *Major Barbara* at the Arts Theatre, received many plaudits.

Between 1930 and 1932, Eric toured the country in several more plays such as *She Stoops to Conquer*, *The Beaux Stratagem*, *The Fake* and *The Sign of the Dove* – the last two performed at the Theatre Royal, Halifax, both in 1931.

Some other reviews stated:
"Mr Portman is a mixture of volatility and passion which marks him as an obvious choice for leading parts as a young lover, whether hero or villain, in entirely modern plays.'

"Eric Portman makes a fine romantic lover. With his rich musical voice he is perhaps the best "Romeo" for years. It is difficult imagining the two parts better cast today."

"Mr Eric Portman in Savon's comedy *The Lion Tamer*, takes one more of those leaps and bounds which are so rapidly making him one of our best actors."

"Eric Portman's notable Don Juan was quite the most distinguished performance of the evening."

"The best performance of all was Eric Portman's as the professional vanquisher of women.'"

"The best performance of all, however, came from Mr Eric Portman as 'Young Marlow'. His suggestion of shyness was artistically conveyed and he made a man of character of what can so easily be made to appear a stick."

"Mr Eric Portman was an entirely admirable 'Marlow' with the most natural stammer in the world."

In April 1932, he was back in Halifax appearing in Edgar Wallace's crime drama: *On The Spot*, playing ruthless Chicago gangster Tony Perelli.

It may have been Eric's influence which brought the theatre company to Halifax at this time, as he was on a salvage job to save the Theatre Royal from possible closure. Dwindling audiences and therefore decreased profits, meant that the theatre's future was hanging in the balance, and a performance of the play in Halifax may have been Eric's attempt to attract new audiences and secure the future of this provincial theatre. By now, he had received acclaim as a stage actor and, although he was not yet an international star, (though he would be in later years, prior to his attempts to 'rescue' Halifax's Grand Theatre from a similar fate), his name, at this time, would still attract the theatre crowds, particularly in Halifax, as he was no doubt considered the 'local lad made good.'

A reporter from the *Halifax Daily Courier and Guardian* of Saturday 23rd April 1932, wrote about his part in the play *On The Spot*:

'As Tony Perelli, Eric Portman has a part the like of which he will probably never have the opportunity of playing again.' (Courtesy of Halifax Courier Ltd) Little did the journalist realise that Eric would, in later years, go on to play many a dark and ruthless character on both stage and screen.

An interesting anecdote at this time, was recounted by local actress Sybil Holroyd. As a member of the twice-nightly repertory company at the Theatre Royal, Halifax, Ms Holroyd had no part in the play, but went to watch the performance on a Monday evening.

She wrote: 'The next morning, I called in at the stage door to be greeted by the producer who informed that the leading lady had had her appendix out in the small hours and I would have to play the part that night! It was then 11am and the curtain went up at 6.30pm. Somehow I managed to learn the part and I played it without the book – and no prompts. Eric made a lovely speech about me at the final curtain.'

Eric's attempts to keep the Theatre Royal open would ultimately fail and it would close its doors for the final time, just two years later. It was fitting, then, that the last play to be performed there, would feature Eric himself, portraying Henry Worthing in Oscar Wilde's comedy *The Importance of Being Earnest*.

More plays followed for Eric over the next year, including *The World of Light, Diplomacy, Midsummer Fires, Chase The Ace*, and he also played the role of Captain Absolute in Richard Brinsley Sheridan's classic comedy *The Rivals*.

On 27th November 1933, it was reported that Eric had an important part in the play *Mrs Siddons*, "…which is to be played at a special matinee in aid of the Personal Service League, at the Apollo Theatre, London. This is a new play by Naomi Royde-Smith, and the title part is to be taken by Miss

Sybil Thorndike. Mr Portman's part is that of Sir Thomas Lawrence, who is an important character in the story." Incidentally, one of the other actors in the play was John Laurie, who would later play Private Frazer in TV's *Dad's Army*.

In 1933, Eric began taking small roles in films, the first being Alexander Korda's largely forgotten musical comedy *The Girl From Maxim's*, which also starred some largely forgotten actors, with the notable exception of Stanley Holloway, who would appear in one of Eric's future movies, when the latter was an established star. Eric's role in the film was so tiny that his name did not appear on the cast list, but I doubt if he simply learned the few lines of his character and left it that. His preparation for each part, even small parts, was exhaustive. He later wrote in his essay on film acting:

'I think that even the small-part actor – the man with but a tiny bit in the film – should study the whole script. The actor must know, must have experienced the sweep of the story in order to be able *to turn on his lamp*. A good film actor studies in advance the entire script of the film as earnestly as he would study a play. The scenes in which the film actor has to appear may be isolated incidents; but, in his mind, the film actor carries the whole of the story. It's no harder for him to give his best in the isolated incident that it is for the stage actor to repeat, at rehearsals, a section of a play. For the good film actor knows his play.'

Although it was a small role in the film – and one that remained uncredited in the cast list – Eric seemed content at that moment to make his name in the theatre, and his parts in stage plays continued pretty much unabated in this period. I can find no record at all of him being out of work at any point: a quite remarkable achievement, I should have thought. I discovered another film Eric appeared in, called *Chu Chin Chow*, made in Germany and directed by Karl Grune. Unless I have got this wrong, the movie appears to be a slapstick comedy, and was apparently based on a British stage musical, inspired by the tale of *Ali Baba and the Forty Thieves*. Eric is billed as playing a 'Conspirator' and you can watch a trailer for the movie at the website www.rottentomatoes.com. I have watched the trailer several times, and been unable to identify Eric in what I assume to be heavy make-up, so if you can spot him amongst the rest of the cast, then you're a better Portman-ite than I am!

Despite his commitment to the stage, the pull of the cinema and all the additional opportunities it offered, was nevertheless appealing to the actor and he appeared in four more films, all released between 1935 and 1936. The first of these was *Maria Marten, or Murder in the Red Barn*, based on a real-life murder case. It starred Tod Slaughter in his film debut playing a murderous country squire, and, even at this early stage, Eric achieved almost star status as a local gypsy – the hero who turns up to save the day.

He later told a journalist: 'I had been on the stage for ten years when I was offered my first film part – the curly-haired gypsy hero in *Maria Marten*. The star was Tod Slaughter. And the picture was quite a success. But not for me! I was, without any question at all, a flop in films.'

I don't think Eric could have been considered a flop in any of his films. As far as I can tell, he never gave a bad performance at all, but of course what he meant was that his appearance in *Maria Marten* did not result in any tantalising offers from film producers. The next film was called *Hyde Park Corner*, named after the location where it was filmed in Central London, and the story involved a police officer investigating a crime in the 1930s, which proves to have its origins in the 1780s, and this provided an early part for another British actor Donald Wolfit. *Old Roses* followed the same year, and was another crime movie in which an elderly man assists the police to solve a murder, but inadvertently uncovers his own criminal past. Eric also appeared in the long-forgotten movies *Hearts of Humanity* and *Abdul the Damned*, and the latter is set in Turkey in 1900, and revolves around an opera singer who gives herself to a villainous sultan, in order to protect her fiance. There are no known reviews from its cinematic release, but there is a comment in *Halliwell's Film Guide*, which describes it as: 'Thorough-going hokum, well produced, which pleased some people in its day.'

Eric returned to the stage, and a press report dated 11th September 1935, reads: 'A former Halifax woman, now residing at Hendon, has sent us news of the Halifax actor Mr Eric Portman, who has been appearing with Marie Ney in *This Desirable Residence.*'

The news takes the form of a personal note appearing in the programme of the Golders Green Hippodrome, the theatre to which the play was moved after its initial run at the Criterion. The report continued: 'While the removal was in progress, the cast was provided with a free week, but Mr Portman, according to the writer of the programme note, had to cancel his holiday in order to fight a duel in a new film part and stayed in Town to take a course of fencing lessons. Now he is engaged on film work as well as a nightly stage performance at the Streatham Hill Theatre, and this means an early morning appearance at the studios for his transformation into an 18th century gallant, and then a rush to Streatham Hill for the last performance of the play in which he is an ambitious scheming clerk of pre-war days. Local cinema-goers have recently had an opportunity of seeing Mr Portman in a minor role in the film *Abdul The Damned*, and evidently his film engagements are now becoming more numerous.'

His next film was *The Cardinal*, a historical drama, starring Matheson Lang, with Eric second-billed as Guiliano De Medici. Although a British movie, it is set in Rome in 1570 and charts a power struggle between Eric's character and one of his rivals.

Despite the actor's view that he was a 'flop' in the movies, Eric must have made some cinematic impression as the heroic figure in *Maria Marten*, as he was now selected to play the hero in another film featuring Tod Slaughter, called *The Crimes of Stephen Hawke*. Here, Eric's character thwarts the murderous plans of the title character, a seemingly kindly man, who leads a double life as a serial killer.

Slaughter specialised in giving over-the-top melodramatic performances as villains. Following *Maria Marten*, he played the title role in *Sweeney Todd: The Demon Barber of Fleet Street* (1936), then followed with the Stephen Hawke film. While Slaughter achieved almost cult status in his films, Eric seemed to immediately vanish without a trace for the time being. And yet, while Slaughter would enjoy a successful career, and was certainly considered a 'star', achieving 'star status' was evidently not Eric's own aim. He would later become the 'problem boy' of British cinema – not due to any disreputable behaviour, but because he simply refused to go for ready-made blockbusters, which may have proven to be 'vehicles' to carry fame-hungry actors to unrivalled stardom. Eric always went for scripts which contained strong characterisations, rather than star turns. In a sense, his sights were set much higher than stardom, and he no doubt viewed that he was still serving his self-appointed apprenticeship in drama.

In his later essay on film-acting, Eric would write: 'Of course it is possible for a clever director to fake a bad screen actor into what seems to be a good performance. By expert cutting, by a very careful selection of exposed footage, it is possible, in certain limited cases, to make a woolly brained actor look as if he were getting down to business. But this is costly. I think we can agree that we want to talk about the good film actor, who can give the director what he wants without wasting time, and not the fake. For the fake, although he may have a short success, can never have a sustained one. His range is bound to be limited to what the cutter and the editor can do with him. After a few pictures, audiences tire of the illusion. Even a magician cannot build an evening's entertainment with one trick. Then, as soon as the box-office receipts fall, the fake is dropped. He is too expensive a trick. And there are plenty of genuine actors who can give audiences the variety that they demand at the fraction of the production-cost of a puppet.'

'The fake probably got his chance because he was fantastically good-looking. The novelty of his good looks was his fortune. When the novelty is spent, the missing qualities which do make a really successful film star, becomes all too evident...'

Eric made one more film called *Moonlight Sonata*. The plot revolves around 'stranded victims of a plane crash who are affected by the art of a famous pianist,' and Eric plays Mario de la Costa, one such survivor. The whole film was meant as a vehicle, or publicity piece, for the famous Polish pianist Ignace Paderewski, and it also featured noted actress and singer Dame Marie Tempest. The exterior scenes were shot at Cragside, the estate of Lord Armstrong, in Northumbria, which doubles for Sweden, where the greater part of the story is set.

The magazine *Variety* wrote: 'Should make good with class audiences.' And the *New York Times* added: 'Dame Marie is a sparkling line-tosser who keeps the script alive when Ignace Paderewski (then aged 77) is not putting it to music.'

In 1936, Eric was back on stage, playing Lord Byron in *Bitter Harvest* by Catherine Turney, which charts Byron's incestuous relationship with his half-sister Augusta. His performance became one of the most memorable and talked-about throughout his stage career, equalled only perhaps by later roles in *Separate Tables*, *His Excellency* and *The Browning Version*.

A report stated that the play "...has been the subject of some controversy on the point of the censor's attitude. The work has at last been licensed, however, and was given its first public performance this week.' It also quoted an unnamed Yorkshire critic who stated that "...Mr Portman's portraiture does not stop at faithful make-up. He offers a moving study of the poet."

Other critics raved:
"Best of all, the play provides a fine, frenzied and full-blown portrait of Byron himself. This is like a Catherine Wheel in the full splendour of its middle course – the play extends only from 1813 to 1816 and we see not the uncertain beginning or the sullen ember of the close. Mr Eric Portman, therefore, plays the poet pyrotechnically and with a splendid range of tones and gestures."

"Here is a fine performance – full-blooded and tempestuous. The make-up is startlingly recognisable, and, though one is not asked to sympathise, one glimpses a forlorn creature at odds with the world. So telling was Mr Portman's portrayal that he somewhat dwarfed the rest of the cast."

James Agate, who refers to Eric as 'a really fine actor' wrote: "Any young man of a Byronic cast can look like Byron. Mr Portman, by means which we cannot discern,

Eric applying his make-up for a theatre production

and of which, as a good actor, he should have no knowledge, conveys the vigour and brilliance of this mind, the melancholy of this temperament and the shoddiness of character which could go hand in hand with sublimity.'

Ivor Brown, commented: "Mr Eric Portman's picture of Byron was a fine interpretation of a finely-written text: he convinced us of genuine power and passion and so held our interest and even our sympathy, while he was behaving with petulance and even brutality."

According to an unnamed critic, Eric's performance as Lord Byron, '...remained fire-stamped on the memory...crippled, tortured, savage and independent... Few

Eric is offered a Hollywood contract with Warner Brothers (Courtesy of the Halifax Courier Ltd

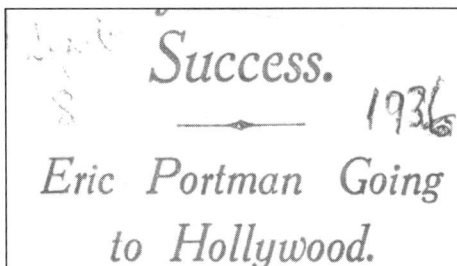

Success. 1936

Eric Portman Going to Hollywood.

From a "Mercury" Special Correspondent.

FLEET STREET, Monday.

ERIC PORTMAN, the young Yorkshire stage actor, has just signed a long-term contract for at least five years with Warner Bros., as a result of his brilliant performance in "Bitter Sweet." He is off next month to Hollywood.

Mr. Portman, who comes from Halifax, is very busy at the moment working at Denham Studios, where he is playing in the new film of the life of Paderewski, starring the famous pianist and Marie Tempest. As soon as it is finished he sets out on this great new enterprise.

Mr. Portman, who was educated at Rishworth School, Halifax, started his professional stage career at the age of 18, when he joined a Shakespearean company under the direction of Robert Courtneidge. The early association has persisted, for he is still more at home in costume than straight parts.

VISITS TO YORKSHIRE.

He attracted the attention of Lilian Baylis, who gave him many parts, including Romeo to Jean Forbes Robertson's Juliet. He has also played with Madeleine Carroll in Basil Dean's production of "The Roof," and acted in one of the last shows that Sir Gerald du Maurier was concerned in before his death.

Although so occupied with the work that has followed from his success, Mr. Portman still finds time to return periodically to Yorkshire, to which he attributes a lot of his success.

Not many months ago Mr. Portman starred with Binnie Hale and Gordon Harker in "Hyde Park Corner." Yorkshire folk, I am sure, will look forward with keen interest to still more films by their own countryman, and wish him every success.

actors could look the part better, or suggest more vividly the raging furnace beneath the marble profile and Hyperion's curls.'

One night, the audience included a talent scout from Hollywood who, like the critics, was impressed with Eric's performance. As a result, he was offered a five-year contract with Warner Brothers, on behalf of producer Hal B. Wallis. I found Eric's name on a passenger list for the ship *Queen Maru*, which arrived in New York on 2nd November 1936. It also read:

Travelling: 2.
Friend's name: Warner Bros.

The young actor arrived in California to honour his movie contract, with the offer of playing the juvenile lead in a new Warner Brothers' movie – Max Rheinhardt's production of *Danton*. But the film was later shelved and was only ever made as a stage play, several years later, and without Eric in the cast. Instead though, he was cast in another movie – *The Prince and the Pauper*.

Everyone must know the story, but here is the basic premise: Two identical boys are born on the same day. One of them is Prince Edward, ready to succeed King Henry VIII, as heir to the throne. The other is Tom Canty, living in poverty and with an abusive father. When their paths cross, they decide to swap identities, and explore each other's lives, but when the Prince returns to the Palace, the guards disbelieve his identity and he is chased off the premises. So begins a host of adventures, in which he is befriended by one Miles Hendon, who protects the boy and ensures he is returned to the palace, just in time for the coronation, and the two boys swap back their identities.

Errol Flynn had star billing, cast as Miles Hendon, twins Billy and Bobby

Mauch played the title roles and Claude Rains featured as the villainous Earl of Hertford. Perhaps Eric Portman was expecting a major role too – or at least a role with a name – but despite his impressive stage performance in *Bitter Harvest*, he was only offered the part of 'First Lord.'

There were many different designs for the movie poster and he appears in small print in some, while in others he is noticeably absent, presumably depending on whether or not he was famous in the countries where the film was released. Although he was fairly well known on the British theatre circuit, he had yet to make his name in the movies on either side of the Atlantic, and was certainly not yet a household name.

The magazine *Variety* described the movie as: 'Lavish but not convincing' and doubted it would be a box office hit, continuing: 'The commercial aspect seems wholly in the timeliness of the Coronation sequence and the name of Errol Flynn. It is not enough.'

Intriguingly, the Internet Movie Database website (www.imdb.com) contains entries on what appear to be two actors named Eric Portman, marked as Eric Portman (I) and Eric Portman (II). The first one details the career of the famous actor, while the second entry lists only one film – *The Singing Marine* – where Eric (II) remains uncredited, playing a soldier stood in the background of a scene, testing a rifle at a fairground, although another source credits him as playing a 'Derelict'.

Was this another actor with the same name? Unfortunately, I have been unable to find a copy of the movie on either DVD or video, and all other attempts to find the true identity of Eric Portman (II) have failed. But since the movie was made by Warner Brothers, while Eric was still under contract with them and resident in California, and that Eric himself later said that he had played various walk-on parts, it is probably safe to assume that this film was one of them.

49

Although he would have got paid as a movie extra, under the terms of his contract, it can't have done much to boost the young actor's confidence. Surely his performance as Byron in *Bitter Harvest* which received so many rave reviews, warranted better roles than 'First Lord' and other unnamed parts as extras?

Eric later commented on this to the *Rotherham Advertiser* in 1937, while visiting his cousins in Thorpe Hesley, near Rotherham, soon after his return to England. He told a reporter that the money is wonderful in Hollywood but the individual is not always used to their full potential. Eric said:

'The writers are worse off than the players. Some of them have been out there for a whole year and never written a line. Their big pay packets were drawn regularly, but they had nothing to do. The players are not as bad as that, but the place is uninteresting after London, and I disliked it so much that I did the unbelievable thing – I broke my contract and came home.' In his later essay on acting, he further commented: 'I don't like being well paid for doing nothing, so I walked out on Hollywood. Yes, you can confirm that in *The Hollywood Reporter*…"Portman walks out on Hollywood." I did a play in New York then came back to London.' (Courtesy of Rotherham Advertiser)

By the time *The Prince and the Pauper* had opened in cinemas on 8th May 1937, Eric had already returned to London and had even reprised his previous stage role, playing Lord Byron in *Bitter Harvest*, at the New Theatre, in London!

He followed this with a role in *The Great Romancer* at the Open Air Theatre, in Regents Park, London, and by November of the same year, he had done another transatlantic hop to play Brutus in *Julius Caesar* at the Broadhurst Theatre in New York. Despite what he viewed as a lack of success in the movies, the critics were still raving about his stage performances, including his part as Brutus, on which Audrey Williamson wrote that Eric Portman was 'livid of face and twisted of mind and gave a performance of sinister power.'

Eric continued to throw himself into a variety of plays, and hopping between Britain and America. Throughout 1938 and 1939, he played Rudolph Boulanger in *Madam Bovary* at the Gate Theatre, London; Crown Prince Rudolph in *Mask of Kings* at the Comedy Theatre, and then returned to the States, playing the role of Richard Dahl in *Give Me Yesterday* at the Guild Theatre, New York.

On Thursday 13th September 1939, it was reported that Eric's father, Matthew, then aged 71 and still running the family business, had been taken ill, and died a fortnight later. He had outlived his wife Alice by twenty-four years. The business continued to be run by Eric's younger brother Leslie.

After the funeral, Eric returned to London to appear as Oliver Farrant in J. B. Priestley's classic *I Have Been Here Before* which is set in a remote hotel and concerns the strange phenomenon of *déjà vu*. 'It was a very brief run,' he recalled later. 'It was a drama about experience repeating itself and reincarnation. I also discovered another reason for the failure. Playing at a theatre, just down the street from us was the Rodgers and Hart musical *Babes in Arms*. There was a song in that show called 'Where or When,' which gave the whole story of our play in about two minutes!'

He also played other roles, frequently alternating between Shakespeare texts and more contemporary dramas, ranging from Mark Anthony in *Julius Caesar*, to Stanley Smith in *Jeannie*, in which he played one of the possible suitors of a Scottish girl who inherits a castle. At Wyndham's Theatre, London, he played the character Blaise Lebel in *The Intruder* by Francois Mauriac.

But here there is a curious aspect to Eric's career. Up to this point, he is dismissive of his previous films. He made at least eleven of them, (including the tiny parts in *The Girl From Maxim's* and *The Singing Marine*) and he only ever refers to two of them – *Maria Marten* and *The Prince and the Pauper* – presumably because each *could* have proved to be his 'big break' on either side of the Atlantic. And yet, in addition to the eleven films for cinematic release, he also appeared in a further seven made-for-TV movies between the period 1938-1939.

These long-forgotten TV productions, with little information available as to their plots, characters, cast and crew, had such titles as: *The Constant Nymph, A Hundred Years Old, The Gamblers, A Night at the Hardcastles* and *The Pelican*. He also appeared in others which were based on stage plays he had appeared in, portraying the very same characters, most notably Captain Absolute in *The Rivals* and Young Marlow in *She Stoops To Conquer.* If we consider the amount of work he did on stage, TV and films by this time, his attitude towards much of his work is either very dismissive or very modest. As is evident from his acting career – with particular reference to his discipline learned in repertory – he obviously pushed himself extremely hard, not only to learn and practice his trade, but based on a quote from an interview in later years: 'He gets paid well for doing a job that he loves.' Perhaps he considered the idea of drawing attention to all his work would sound a mite boastful.

Opportunities in TV as an emerging medium were plentiful and so, even at this early stage in his career, Eric managed to add a third string to his bow which had started with theatre and films.

Later he would say of TV work: 'You spend about three weeks rehearsing, all day and every day. You work terribly hard and travel to far-flung parts of London for run-throughs in parish halls and places. You appear before the cameras on The Night and it's a most alarming experience. For all this, you are paid – if you are the star of the show – about a hundred guineas.'

'I say it is a very wonderful medium – one that no actor can afford to ignore. Why am I so positive? (There is) an immense feeling of satisfaction. TV is so very stimulating because it is a wonderful medium for actual and real character playing. More so than either the theatre and films by themselves. You can express far more than in any other medium, particularly in the close-ups, which come within the continuity of your performance – not, as in a film, days or weeks after you have done other parts of the scene. Television is a tonic. It is also a challenge. Consider for a moment what is required of the actor during a performance. He has to draw upon film experience to act before no audience, other than staring at preoccupied technicians (it's frightening). He draws upon film experience again for the volume of his acting – the voice and so on. All the time, the TV actor is aware that he is in an unfamiliar medium, but cannot see the finished results. He has no real idea of how he is coming over. I wonder, though, is it because they won't face up to a challenge that more screen actors don't try TV plays? They ought to have a try at TV. Most of them have had a background of theatre experience as well as filming experience. That, as I've said, is an ideal combination for TV work. After all, trying TV should be no more difficult a task for today's film actors than was trying sound for the silent film players of yesterday.'

Years later, he told a journalist that TV acting is '…alright when whatever one does is pre-filmed. Making a 'live' appearance is a rather nerve-wracking business; people can make such shocking errors when playing live.'

As for his experience of moviemaking, which he was unsatisfied with, and also alluding to his much acclaimed stage career and recent additional opportunities in television, Eric stated: 'That decided it. No more movies for me. The war started and I was acting in *The Intruder* at Wyndhams, in which I was lucky to receive a good press. Again, I suddenly received further movie offers, but I refused them all....except one.'

CHAPTER 3

LIFE BEGINS AT 40

For Eric Portman, life really *did* begin at forty, when he was offered a role that was to catapult him to stardom.

Says the actor: 'Michael Powell and Emeric Pressburger wanted me to act the part of a Nazi in a film called *The 49th Parallel* – and this was so different from the romantic stage and screen roles I had played, that I became immediately intrigued.'

Pressburger had come up with the basic premise for *The 49th Parallel*: 'I think we wreck a German submarine somewhere in Canada and then follow the survivors all across Canada and that way we shall see Canada, and we've got a good suspense story.'

The plot centres around six survivors of a Nazi U-Boat, led by Eric's character – sadistic and ruthless commander Lieutenant Hurth – in the early years of the Second World War, as they attempt to escape across Canada. The film feels like a series of episodes, with each one showing how the survivors encounter – violently in some cases – a variety of Canadians. Each of the survivors are picked off one by one, until there is only one remaining – Hurth himself – who wants to flee the country and seek safe haven at the German Embassy, in America, because the States, at the time, was neutral and presumably happy to allow Nazis into the country! When

Hurth successfully reaches the Canadian/American border, he surrenders his gun to the Customs Official, but the character Brock (Raymond Massey) suggests that Hurth is sent back to Canada – which he then is.

Pressburger described it as like Agatha Christie's plot for *And Then There Were None* – without the whodunit element, although in hindsight, the premise had much more in common with later movies like *The Towering Inferno* and *The Poseidon Adventure*, where a group of survivors, as an ensemble cast, dodge danger after danger, attempting to make their way to safety. The title is taken from the 49th Parallel north, which marks part of the border between Canada and the USA, which Hurth reaches after his escape.

Michael Powell hoped to receive funding from the MoI (Ministry of Information) to make *The 49th Parallel*. In February 1940, it was reported to the Cabinet that thirty-two films, all documentaries, had received funding and had been completed – all of them intended to help the propaganda effort, with each of them showing 'various aspects of our part in the war.'

The previous films made by Powell and Pressburger were largely 'propaganda films' – not produced purely for entertainment purposes but with each one having an underlying and important statement which would influence a change for the greater good in the real world. And certainly during the Second World War, propaganda films existed to reassure British audiences, and to prevent apathy, about the British war effort, while others were meant for consumption by foreign audiences, particularly those resident in the British Empire, for the same reasons. The MOI had persuaded nearly all of the film companies to produce documentaries which presented the British government's war aims and efforts in a favourable light.

The Films Division of the Ministry of Information was rumoured to be touting for suggestions for further films and Michael Powell recalls how a colleague told him '…the government definitely wants to back films. They will even put government money into (them), if we can't raise the money elsewhere.'

Originally, Kenneth Clark was put in charge of the Films Division and suggested Michael Powell make a film about minesweepers, but Powell and Pressburger already had their own idea about Canada's entry into the war – a story which became *The 49th Parallel*. Pressburger later remarked: 'Goebbels considered himself an expert on propaganda, but I thought I'd show him a thing or two!'

Powell's aim was to make a movie which would sway opinion in the USA, which was still neutral at the time, and had not yet joined the Allied Forces against the Nazis. He said: 'I hoped it might scare the pants off the Americans (and thus bring them into the war).' Therefore, Hurth's attempt to seek sanctuary at the German Embassy in the USA, following his murder spree in Canada, would no doubt make the Americans sit up and rethink whether they really wanted to remain neutral to the impending Nazi threat. And Kenneth Clark said there was room for '…a first-class feature film developing as an exciting story, about the history of the growth of freedom, referring to the American parallel and stimulus in order to give it appeal to the US audiences.'

From April to September 1940, the Films Division were already contemplating funding at least two full-length feature films: 'One for Canada on the NW Mounted Police and one for South Africa on the life of General Botha'. The budget for these films would be met "…from the Film's sub-head of the Ministry vote, amounting to £500,000 in 1940." But luckily for Powell, neither of the proposed films had yet reached the stage where accurate costing was available. He realised that, if they were quick, and travelled to Canada to search for possible movie locations, enabling them to do a costing, and then returned forthwith with a full-scale storyline, then the odds in favour of securing funding were certainly in their favour. So Powell, Pressburger, and three others travelled to Canada.

The team returned with a more accurate estimate of the cost and what the film would eventually look like, and promises were gained from various actors that would be prepared to appear in it, including Laurence Olivier, Elizabeth Bergner, Leslie Howard, Raymond Massey and Anton Walbrook. As it transpired, Olivier, Howard and Massey all worked for half their normal fee because they felt that it was an important propaganda film, and Walbrook donated half of his fee to the International Red Cross.

By this time, there was a new Minister of Information, Duff Cooper, who took a considerable interest in the project, evidently thinking that circumstances warranted an increase in the propaganda effort, and he was instrumental in persuading the Treasury to release funding for the movie.

Powell's original choice of actor to play Lieutenant Hurth was Esmond Knight who had appeared in other films by Powell and Pressburger, but he had already joined the Royal Navy at the outbreak of the war, as had another early choice, Michael Redgrave. Also, John Mills was an early contender for the role, after he had been invalided out of the army, though he had already agreed to appear in another film.

When looking for a replacement, Powell remembered seeing Eric Portman playing a Yorkshire character in the play *Jeannie*, in which actress Barbara Mullen had also attracted attention from movie producers for the first time. The play had been performed in a small theatre holding only about eighty people, so it was certainly not a major London production but, even so, as a journalist pointed out: 'Eric Portman is, therefore, another actor who explodes the myth that the film-makers do not know what is going on in the theatre or who is up-and-coming.' But this is evident anyway, as Eric's

Hollywood contract came about as a direct result of a talent scout seeing his performance in *Bitter Harvest*.

Despite his experience in movie-making, Eric was certainly nervous about taking on another film role, particularly after his recent decision to quit them. He evidently considered that any long-term success for him would arrive as a stage actor. He said: 'I had a background of classical and Shakespearean acting and ambitions along classical lines; you know, the tights pulled over the shapely leg, the dark ringlets, the profile against the purple curtain.'

When Michael Powell offered the role to Eric, the actor recalled: 'I had to decide on it almost immediately and leave for Canada in a matter of hours. I had other important stage offers which I was on the point of accepting, for I realised if I did appear in this film, then it would take me to Canada, away from the London theatre, for a dangerously long time. The theatre has a remarkably short memory.'

'When I first took the part, I asked Michael Powell if I could play it absolutely straight; that is, seriously and sincerely without making it a caricature of a Nazi. Nazism has ceased to be funny. It is no longer a joke; indeed, it is extremely dangerous.'

So Eric accompanied the movie-makers to Canada, and as the actor leaned on the ship's rail, looking back at the shore, he said to a friend: 'Well, we are off on a big job. I wonder if it – and we – will be successful?'

'With fifteen members of the film, I went to Baffin Land,' the actor later recalled to a journalist and, while on location there, Eric wrote a letter to his younger brother Leslie and wife Alice, still running the family business, back in Halifax. The letter was dated July 24th 1940, and scribbled on notepaper headed 'Lake O'Hara Lodge (A Canadian Pacific Mountain Resort) Hector, B,C.' He wrote:

My dear Alice, Les and all of you,
Well, here I am in the middle of the Canadian Rockies – about 5000 miles from home! I was so sorry not to be able to see you before I came away or even to let you know I was coming until the last minute. The fact is I had no idea that I was starting off on this wild journey until the night before myself – so you can guess what a state I was in – no real decision – nothing packed of course – no arrangements made about the flat or anything. It was a very great struggle to make up my mind at all to leave England just now. For the first minute or two, of course, it seemed to be a splendid idea – a long three months' journey through every part of Canada – just when one was so worried at home. But that mood lasted for no time at all, and I can't tell you how unhappy I was when finally I had only about 8 hours to decide and I was pushed into the plan and I found myself on the train for Liverpool. The voyage was most difficult too. We were carrying a great number of children. The parting at Liverpool was simply heartbreaking. To see the 'ordinary' Englishmen break down in desperate tears was terrifying. Life can be very cruel, I think. Since we got to Montreal I'm afraid I haven't been at all myself. There is so little authentic news here – a great deal of lying, it seems to me, in the papers, so I have decided not to read them. It is too distressing.'

'I pray that things will not become too awful before I get back. We are

Eric writes to his family, while on location in Canada, filming *The 49th Parallel* supposed to be home by the 30th September. I know now that I would rather bear anything in England than be in this safer, but lonely – tragically lonely – country.'

'The film is rather interesting – it is sponsored by the Government – that's why we were able to get out of the country, of course. From Montreal we went to Banff, quite a lovely mountainous place – from there to this 'Rockies' place – ravishingly lovely – a bright emerald green lake surrounded by enormous mountains with perpetual snow – exciting in a way but alarming too. One feels about the size of a mouse – and just about as important to the universe. You'll be amused to hear that we travel everywhere by horseback. Naturally I was a bit shaken when I realised this was to be the case, but I am now just expert – galloping up mountain trails – literally – over rushing torrents and so on. Incredible and strangely enough quite enjoyable. Tomorrow we go back to Banff again on horseback, then on to Winnipeg – then back to Montreal – Nova Scotia – Newfoundland – then we charter a boat to take us to Hudson's Bay! I suppose it's all right! My "permanent" address while in Canada is: c/o Ortus Films, Windsor Hotel, Montreal.

And I do hope that if anybody has a minute to spare you'll write to me. I feel so very 'cut off' and so very anxious about you all. Give my love please to all the children – and to you, too – and Irene and Clifford. I send all my heartfelt wishes for all good things,
      Ever affectionate,
      Eric.

I found a record noting that Eric and the others returned from Canada by ship, *Duchess of Richmond*, which was owned by the shipping line Canadian Pacific, which docked at Liverpool on 26th October 1940.

The actor later told a journalist: 'We returned (from Canada) with wonderful background scenes, in which I appeared in not one scene – but many. No story had been prepared for this film till our return to London where two famous stars, Laurence Olivier and Leslie Howard, were signed to appear as stars of the film.'

The cast and crew had already shot a lot of the movie, when the Government's 13th Select Committee produced the results of its inquiry into the affairs of the MoI and the Films Division. The Committee had decided that there were difficulties of employing feature films 'as an instrument of propaganda', and their report recommended that the emphasis should be put upon the newsreels (rather than documentaries or feature films) since the select committee considered they were 'the most important for propaganda purposes.'

But Powell's initial decision to act quick and start on location had saved the day as the film shooting was too far advanced to have been affected by this decision.

The shooting in Canada had not posed too many problems, as Powell recalled: 'Almost immediately after we landed (in Canada) my chief of construction, Sid Streeter, started to build the submarine in Halifax (Nova Scotia) while I was already shooting; I think we started in the mid-west. We'd roughed the whole script out and then Emeric started to write the actual script with dialogue, with co-writer Rodney Ackland. They started on the first episode while I went to shoot the rest of the stuff off-the-cuff. We had to catch the harvest for the Hutterite sequence, then I had to shoot the stuff in the Rockies and then go up to Hudson Bay and round the Laborador Coast to get the submarine scenes and the landing at the Hudson Bay post. All before it was too late, because if you're too late in Hudson Bay, the ice can be early. It was all working against time, but as we had complete control ourselves, and nobody to argue with, we brought it all off. When we came back to England, the Blitz was on. We had shot Raymond Massey's sequence with Eric Portman in a little documentary studio in Montreal, because (Massey) was already in the Forces and couldn't come over to the UK.'

Eric later recalled: 'It was a bit of luck that I starred in this film. I was chosen to play a minor part in a single scene with Raymond Massey. It was not till the film was finished that it was discovered that the one role which connected the episodes and tied the film together was mine. Leslie Howard insisted that in these circumstances I should be co-starred.'

Although there were no serious hiccups while shooting the film in Canada, the problems began when the production cast and crew returned to England, as recounted in *Documentary News Letter* in December 1940:

'The Press lately has been full of *The 49th Parallel*, a feature film on Canada, partly financed by the Films Division of the MoI. This film has gone wrong largely because the star, Austrian-born Elizabeth Bergner, refuses to return to London to complete the studio scenes, (*presumably because of the bombing). Among the general sensation-mongering, two points have been overlooked: the idea of the original script was, and remains, a good one. In spite of Miss Bergner's absence, there is, as yet, no reason to suppose, either that the film will not be finished, or that it will not be a success.'

'This hurdle would require a replacement actress, re-shooting of certain scenes and more money to achieve this. Most of the problems were solved. Glynis Johns was engaged to replace Elizabeth Bergner for the studio work. David Lean, the editor, (*later a film director himself) cleverly managed to retain some of the location material done with Bergner – the long shots in which her features could not be clearly discerned – and J. Arthur Rank was cajoled into putting £60,000 (to match the £60,000 that the MoI had invested) into the production. But the whole process did take an inordinate amount of time. As a result, the film was not completed and ready, until well over a year-and-a-half after that initial meeting with Kenneth Clark of the Films Division of the MoI.'

Eric told a journalist: 'When it is released it is going to have a great influence on American public opinion concerning the war. When we were in Hudson's Bay, I couldn't help thinking that there was nothing in the story which could not actually happen.'

As Eric said, by the time the cast and crew had returned from Canada, the London blitz was on and, having failed to see his family before he had left for Canada, he wasted no time in visiting them on his return. It was, however, a short visit to Halifax, for he had promised to raise money for the war effort in Southport, Lancashire, and was shortly to take the play *Jeannie* on tour for ENSA, performing it to soldiers at military camps around the UK entertaining the troops, as many major stars did during the war.

On his return to London, he wrote a letter addressed to his sister-in-law Alice, living at number 20 Chester Road with his brother Leslie Portman and their sons John and Michael. The letter is handwritten on notepaper, with the letterhead: Orford House, Rawlings Street, SW3, where Eric had a flat.

It read:

My Dear Alice,
Was so glad to have your letter. The trip (to Halifax) was much too short and I disliked very much having to go to Southport where I found myself billed:

"The Jewish Effort
With
EP!"

And was summoned by them exclusively over the weekend. Not a Gentile in sight! It was interesting in a way but very tiring. They had arranged four appearances in one day! Nothing like getting value out of people. They got £1000 at the Concert however so I suppose it was worth while.

I enjoyed the Mayor's Ball and the party so much…though I felt pretty tired next day. Old age creeping up on. I wish I had been able to see Michael (Eric's nephew) but hope to next time. I'll write to him at school.

I have to start out on an E.N.S.A Tour of the Camps again on Monday next – rather dreary but one musn't grumble. In a way it's quite amusing but I hope the weather will be a little warmer. It's freezing here at the moment and the raids are most unpleasant. I'm enclosing a few photographs (all I've got I'm afraid). They've stopped doing them; so that all my poor fans are getting little polite "regrets."

I'm glad to hear Les is well. Give him my best love.

Please write again soon. With love to you and the children.

      Ever Yours,

         Eric

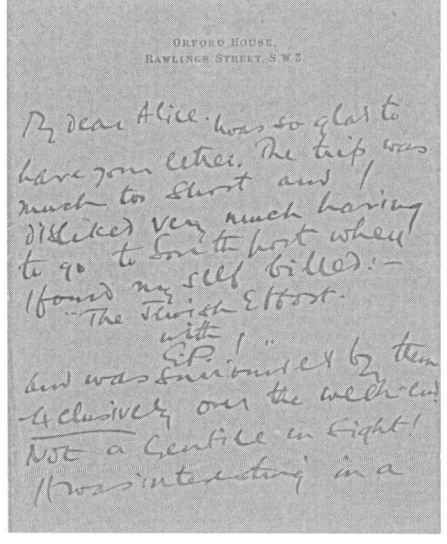

Eric's letter to his family on a UK tour to raise money

The premier of *The 49th Parallel* was held at the Odeon, Leicester Square, London, on 8th October 1941 and the film was put on general release in Britain from 24th November that year.

The critics were generally favourable: 'Tense action…excellent performances. An absorbing and exciting film!' wrote one critic the where another remarked: 'This is an important and effective film. Opening scenes promise much, and it lives up to expectations. Every part, to the smallest bits, is magnificently played…' Another review described the film as: '(an) Episodic, effective propaganda piece which develops some nice Hitchcockian touches and allows a range of star actors to make impact.' One critic wrote: 'The sense of landscape and figures passing through it remains authoritatively dynamic,' and another viewed it as: '…an admirable piece of work from every point of view.'

Several continuity problems were noted, including the attack sequence in Hudson Bay, where the Royal Canadian Air Force bombers inexplicably change from Lockheed Hudsons to Douglas Digby aircraft in mid-scene!

It has been argued that *The 49th Parallel* changed Eric Portman's fortunes. But although it was a great film – still is, in my opinion – I would argue that it was Eric Portman who changed Eric Portman's fortunes. After all, it was he who had convinced Michael Powell it would be better to play the Nazi as a human being – not a stereotypical Nazi. Would the film have been so successful, had Lieutenant Hurth been portrayed as a non-descript, soulless, fanatical, almost robotic villain in a Nazi uniform? Part of the shock to the audience was that Hurth was not only sane, but that he also passionately believed in the ideals of the Nazis.

The film was released a month before the Japanese attacked Pearl Harbour and America joined the Allied Forces shortly afterwards, so we will never know for sure how much the film influenced America to ditch its neutrality. The film was nominated for Best Picture and Best Screenplay at the Academy Awards, and Emeric Pressburger won an award for Best Story. The British Film Institute ranked it as the 63rd most popular film with

British audiences, based on cinema attendance of 9.3 million in the UK.

Some years later in June 1947, Peter Noble interviewed Eric and the article was entitled: 'When portrayed by Eric Portman – even the Nazis seemed Nice'.

Noble wrote: 'It has been suggested that Portman completely stole the film from the rest of the distinguished cast and it reportedly earned him …thousands of plaudits in both England and America. Perhaps it was a reaction against the stereotyped Nazis which, up to then, had appeared with Teutonic inevitability on the wartime screen, or perhaps it was the particularly English feeling of sympathy for the underdog as Hurth is chased through Canada and finally captured after the rest of his crew had been killed.'

Whatever the reason for its success, the executives of Warner Brothers were no doubt kicking themselves over and around the Hollywood Hills for having under-used the actor in his contract, so much so, that he had done the unthinkable – walked out on Hollywood. But then Eric wasn't aiming to be a star. He just wanted to play interesting characters to the best of his ability and get paid for doing something he loved.

On Tuesday November 4th 1941, the *Halifax Daily Courier and Guardian* reported how Eric had

Eric attends a civic reception in his honour while promoting *The 49th Parallel* in local cinemas (Courtesy of the Halifax Courier Ltd)

been besieged by autograph hunters at the Odeon cinema, Halifax, where he was attending the screening of *The 49th Parallel.*

Mr Portman said: 'I, as a Yorkshireman, formed the definite opinion that the picture would never be finished until Mr Powell, who had the courage of his conviction concerning the film and his co-directors, furnished another £100,000 – again with more hostile criticism. I don't think I need say any more. The film has had an amazing reception in this country so far, and is having a long run in London.'

Eric recalled that he was very much impressed with the hospitality of Yorkshire-born expatriates, whom he met while filming in Canada. "Many of them had been there 20 or 30 years," he said, "But they were still Yorkshire"!'

Following the screening, he was introduced onstage and expressed thanks for the great reception, adding that he hoped local people would not think that he was really so revolting as the part of the ruthless Nazi he played in the film. A journalist added that Mr Portman would shortly be returning to the theatre (or 'legitimate stage' as the journalist put it), and that he had agreed to lend his services to promoting local charitable appeals for a week.

Amongst the other locations where Eric attended regional premieres of the movie, included Newcastle, and Alan Sidney-Wilmot recalled to me his brief meeting with Eric at Newcastle Odeon Theatre, where his father R. C. Sidney-Wilmot was the manager. Although Alan exchanged a few words with the actor, he was only twelve years old at the time and unfortunately doesn't remember the conversation! Again, as in Halifax, *The 49th Parallel* was playing to a full house and the *Newcastle Chronicle* stated how Eric appeared on stage at the interval and received several guests including the local Mayor and Mayoress.

Alan recalls: 'At this time, this was a key Odeon Theatre and was visited by many film stars for personal appearances, and my wife and I met most of them. During the war, there was a Sunday concert to keep morale up.'

The 49th Parallel boosted Eric Portman's career and made him instantly recognisable to many who encountered him – not only to the somewhat limited theatre audiences, but now also to the nation's many cinema-goers too.

Edward Motteram told me of an incident he heard about, in 1942, when Eric and fellow *49th Parallel* star Leslie Howard were walking through Trafalgar Square and were accosted by the 'lunchtime crowd'. Says Mr Motteram: 'They signed a few autographs and then, to the delight of the fans, took it in turns to recite speeches from Shakespeare, before continuing on their way!'

Eric was obviously relieved about the success of the movie. 'I had twice been a film flop.' (Despite his several other films, he was probably referring to his first major role in *Maria Marten*, and what he initially thought was his big break in *The Prince and the Pauper*).

'Could I break the jinx?' said Eric. 'I took a chance. You know the result.'

Shortly afterwards, he received a cable offering him a part in the stage version of *Madame Bovary*, in New York, co-starring Constance Cummings, which he accepted, and stayed for the run. Eric told a journalist: "At this moment, I have been asked to do a film with her, probably starting in January (1942), but definite plans have not been made."

He was probably discussing the 1942 movie *Thunder Rock*, with Barbara Mullen, but Eric did not feature in it. He either decided against it, or lost out, to Michael Redgrave.

Eric continued: 'I have received some startling offers since my Nazi role. And I have just finished a film by the same director – *One of Our Aircraft Is Missing* – in which a British air crew bale out over Holland.'

Asked if he preferred the films to the stage, Eric didn't choose between them, but commented: 'The technique of the film, rather than action, makes the work incredibly interesting. The merest flicker of an eyelid can convey so much – the difference between thinking and expressing the part.'

In a poll run by the *Motion Picture Herald*, in 1942, Eric was voted among the first ten top money-making stars in British productions and he remained on the list for four years running.

The 1942 movie, *One of Our Aircraft is Missing*, marked the fourth collaboration between writers/directors/producers Michael Powell and Emeric Pressburger. Like Eric's previous film appearance, it was made under the authority of the Government's Ministry of Information, with a view to boosting British morale through the hard years of the Second World War.

The plot involves the crew of a British bomber who bail out over Nazi-occupied Holland – one of them who goes missing. Eric plays one of the crew, a character who is, to an extent, a real-life version of himself. Tom Earnshaw is the son of a Yorkshire woollen man, also from Halifax, and there are several references to Eric's home town in the movie. The Dutch people, led by Else Meertens (Pamela Brown), firstly interrogate the crew, before locating the sixth crew member, and then help them to escape back to England. Despite some of the Dutch having being accidentally killed in British bombing raids, they still agree to help the British airmen, even at great personal risk to themselves. No doubt, this was the element which appealed to the Ministry of Information, hoping to boost British morale emphasising that Britain had many allies, who did not bear them grudge or ill will.

The cast also included Googie Withers, Hugh Burden, Roland Culver, Robert Beatty, and Peter Ustinov in his film debut. Co-producer Michael Powell also appeared in a minor role as a Despatching Officer.

The movie received Academy Award Nominations for both Powell and Pressburger. While the latter won two for his input on *The 49th Parallel* and a nomination for another movie, *The Red Shoes*, Powell was only nominated this one time – and never won. The film was cut by twenty minutes for its original American release, and Powell decided to use no soundtrack music. He wanted to make the film as 'naturalistic' as possible, and relied on sounds that would have been heard by the characters, such as birdsong. Various later productions played on the title of the movie, including a comedy film made in 1975, called *One of Our Dinosaurs is Missing*, with the cast featuring Peter Ustinov and Hugh Burden, who were in the original Powell and Pressburger film.

One review of the movie described it as: 'An effective propaganda piece which starts vigorously but gets bogged down in talk.' A journalist wrote of Eric: 'This part is just the reverse of his role in *The 49th Parallel* and will convince his many admirers that he is not the villainous creature known in that film.'

Uncensored was another film released in the same year. A wartime thriller directed by Anthony Asquith for Gainsborough Pictures, it was written by Rodney Ackland and the playwright Terence Rattigan. Based on an original novel by Oscar Millard, it concerns the staff of anti-Nazi newspaper *La Libre Belgique* (Free Belgium), and Eric plays the editor, Andre Delange, who used to publish the newspaper prior to the Nazi occupation of Belgium. But when the Germans invade the country, he and his workers decide to revive it. Delange and his team, including Julie Lanvin (Phyllis Calvert), resurrect it and secretly circulate copies, but when the Nazis discover its existence, they offer a reward to anyone who identifies those responsible. Charles Neels, (played by Peter Glenville) is Delange's business partner and, unhappy with their business relationship, and jealous of Delange and

Julie's burgeoning romance, he betrays them to the Nazis. Although the two evade capture, the rest of the team are arrested and imprisoned. Then the race is on for our two heroes to produce and circulate a new edition of the newspaper. When the Nazis see this, they feel foolish at having arrested what appear to be the wrong people, and so release the staff of the newspaper, who then rejoin Delange and Julie to continue publishing it.

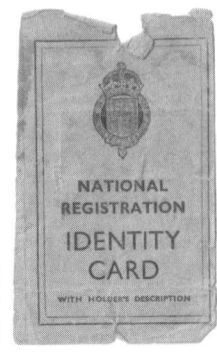

Eric Portman's Identification Card from World War II

Despite his growing opportunities in the movie industry at this time, Eric was still seeking theatrical roles and went on tour playing the title role in *Uncle Harry*.

This play, written by Thomas Job, tells the story of Harry Quincey, a mild-mannered bachelor dominated by his two spinster sisters, Lettie and Hester, who call him 'Uncle' Harry. Furious at them for destroying his chance of marrying local girl Lucy Forrest, he tricks Lettie into buying some poison and serving it to Hester in some cocoa, who drinks it and dies. Lettie is sentenced to die for the murder and, to his dismay, Lucy will no longer have anything to do with him. So Harry confesses to the crime, but the authorities think he is just bluffing to try and save his sister, and Lettie refuses to reveal the truth. When Lettie is executed for the crime, Harry is doomed to a life of loneliness and disgrace.

The reviewer Richard Lockridge described it as: 'An admirably sinister murder play, slightly diabolical in its ingenuity and warranted to make the timid look hereafter with uneasy suspicion on all quiet little men.' Again, the play toured the country, one such venue being back in Halifax. When he appeared onstage after the performance, he received a civic reception and presented a donation to the Halifax Royal Infirmary. The local Mayor Alderman J. Oddy said it particularly pleased him to welcome Eric to Halifax, as he had known the actor's family for many years and Eric told the crowd of well-wishers that he looked upon the reception in his native town as a great honour.

Eric further commented that a general revival of the theatre was apparent. The signs, he said, were especially marked in London, and were also in evidence in the provinces. However, this comment seems in contradiction to what actually happened, particularly to theatres in Halifax, and may be viewed in hindsight as vain optimism. Despite the actor's best efforts, the town's Theatre Royal had lost audiences and closed to the public eight years earlier. This was the first casualty of dwindling audiences and, as Eric was to discover in later years, it would not be the last.

Eric also said that following his portrayal of the title character in the *Uncle Harry*, playing in London, he would return to film work in the early autumn to complete his contract with the Gainsborough Film Company. He also mentioned that he may be set to play the 'Dauphin' in the film *Henry the Fifth* with an all-star cast, including Laurence Olivier and Ralph Richardson. As it turned out, though, he either lost out – or decided against it – and the part of the Dauphin was played by Irish actor Max Adrian. Perhaps this was a conscious decision, that Eric should make the most of his success on the screen and avoid playing second- or third-fiddle to other actors, such as Olivier and Richardson, as he had done with Errol Flynn in *The Prince and the Pauper*. Perhaps his agent advised him to go for as many starring roles as possible to cement his name in the industry as what is known these days as a 'Celebrity A-lister'.

In his article *The Mark of Cain: Eric Portman and Stardom*, Dr Andrew Spicer states that: 'Portman temporarily abandoned his stage career at this point, going under contract with J. Arthur Rank Organisation but working with individual producers who were sensitive to his capabilities. However, his reluctance to appear in parts he thought unworthy of his talent led him to reject the part of Lord Rohan in *The Man in Grey* (Leslie Arliss, 1941) the role that shot James Mason to stardom...and his relations with Box Productions reportedly deteriorated when he refused to appear in *The Brothers* (1947) which meant that the title role in *The Bad Lord Byron* (1949) went to Dennis Price.' (Courtesy of Andrew Spicer)

And yet, out of his next four films, he was the top-billed actor in two of them, shared star-billing with John Mills in a third, and was part of an ensemble cast in the fourth.

Despite his comments about an equal appeal for both the stage and films, Eric kept busy with film-making and 1943 saw the release of four further movies. In *Squadron Leader X*, directed by Lance Comfort, he plays Erich Kohler, a Luftwaffe pilot on a mission to bomb the Belgian city of Ghent. First he must fly over the city and bomb it, then bale out of his plane wearing an RAF uniform. His mission is to befriend the Belgians and convince them that the British are responsible for bombing civilian targets in Belgium. However, the plan comes unstuck when he is accosted by the Belgian Resistance, who believe they are helping him by smuggling him 'back' to England with some RAF pilots whose planes have been shot down over Belgium. Once in England, he seeks help from British nurse Barbara Lucas (played by Ann Dvorak) who used to be a Nazi sympathiser, together with a couple who are reluctantly being used as informers, for their family in Germany are being threatened by the Nazis.

Due to his failed mission, he is ruthlessly hunted by MI5 agent Milne (played by Walter Fitzgerald) and ruthless Gestapo officer Schultz (played by Henry Oscar). Although Kohler manages to escape by stealing an RAF plane, intending to fly back to Germany, he is shot down by German pilots who mistake him for their enemy.

The film got some rave reviews. *The Picturegoer* declared it: 'One of the best spy melodramas yet made'. *The Monthly Film Bulletin* described a movie cast 'that is of the highest order' and noted that the story was 'exciting, well produced, with tremendous attention to detail.' *The Cinema* pointed out that the air-sequences, which were made with official Air Ministry cooperation, were among the most action-packed and breath-taking ever screened. Though another review stated that it was a 'tall war story with dreary romantic trimmings.'

Eric Portman plays Erich Kohler in the great missing movie *Squadron Leader X* (© RKO Radio Pictures)

Unfortunately for Portman fans, *Squadron Leader X* is ranked as one of Cinema's 'lost' movies. There is no record of it ever being shown again after its original release, and it is included on the British Film Institute's '75 Most Wanted' list of British feature films. In fact, it is named as the third 'most wanted' film of all time, just behind Alfred Hitchcock's *The Mountain Eagle* and Michael Powell's *Two Crowded Hours*. During my research, I heard a rumour that the owner of an American media company either had a copy – or the original itself – though at the moment it remains a rumour and nothing more. If this could be found and copied, the film would be of interest not only to Portman fans and aficionados of British war films, but also to those who admire the work of director Lance Comfort, as his films are revered by many people.

Another of Eric's films at this time was *We Dive At Dawn*, where he plays Seaman Hobson, a moody and unpopular member of a submarine crew, but who eventually risks his life to save the day.

Directed by Anthony Asquith for Gainsborough Pictures, and filmed in Britain at the studios of the Gaumont British Picture Corporation, it tells the story of the crew of Royal Navy submarine 'Sea Tiger'. Lieutenant Taylor (John Mills) and the crew are given a week's leave and the first part of the film focuses on the dilemmas of two crew members: Hobson (Eric Portman) and Corrigan (Niall MacGinnis) as they head home; Hobson attempting to save his marriage, and Corrigan who is reluctant to get married.

However, they are called back from their leave on a new mission as the Sea Tiger has been assigned the top secret mission of sinking the Nazi's new battleship, the Brandenburg, before it enters the Kiel Canal to begin its manoeuvres in the Baltic Sea. After an unscheduled and frantic underwater cat-and-mouse game with the Brandenburg, during which they fire torpedoes at the Brandenburg – not knowing if they hit their mark – the crew of the Sea Tiger realise they don't have enough fuel to return to England, after their unscheduled detour. Taylor decides that the crew should 'abandon ship' and make for a Danish island nearby, but Hobson has another plan. He knows the island and can speak fluent German. He volunteers to go ashore in a German uniform, then find some fuel and return it to the ship and as Sea Tiger refuels, Hobson and the crew hold off the Nazi soldiers. When they return to base in England, they hear that they sank the Brandenburg. Waiting for them on the shore are Hobson's wife and son, and Corrigan's son, and the two seamen receive a heroes' welcome.

Although *Halliwell's Film Guide* described it as a 'fairly routine war suspenser', I found it to be a balanced mixture of action and characterisation. If it was just about the characters, then it would be nothing more than a wartime character drama. Whereas if it was just the about the submarine's mission, without the sub-plots involving Hobson's and Corrigan's relationships back home, then the review above would be an accurate description. And yet, in my opinion, with the two elements combined, it makes for an entertaining and satisfying action drama.

Millions Like Us, released in 1943, was intended as another propaganda film, and is set in a wartime aircraft factory, filmed at Gainsborough Studios for Gainsborough Pictures. Directed by Sidney Gilliat and Frank Lauder, the story charts the lives of several characters who work in a munitions factory, helping the war effort. Most of the film centres around shy Celia Crowson (Patricia Roc) and her blossoming romance with equally shy flight sergeant Fred Blake, played by Gordon Jackson in a rare co-starring role. (Although Jackson appeared in smaller roles in many other films, he would later became a household name to TV audiences playing the butler Hudson in *Upstairs, Downstairs* and George Cowley in *The Professionals*). The couple get married and go on honeymoon in a south-west coastal resort, but find the landscape Celia remembered has been much-changed with a minefield and barbed wire on the beach, as protection against an expected Nazi invasion. Tragically, Fred is killed in a bombing raid, and the film ends on a sombre note, with Celia being comforted by friends as they hear Fred's squadron flying over the factory, enroute to their next bombing mission and Celia displays a proud and defiant smile.

Eric Portman plays works supervisor Charlie Forbes and his character's contribution is more of a sub-plot, particularly concerning one of Celia's fellow workers, upper-middle-class Jennifer Knowles (played by Anne

Crawford). Jennifer causes friction amongst the workforce and particularly with Charlie Forbes, although eventually they warm to each other, and by the end of the movie, there is a romance and impending marriage, albeit a highly improbable one, or so it seemed to me.

The film includes a number of well-known actors such as Megs Jenkins, Moore Marriott (who played in a number of early Will Hay comedies), and the film marks the first appearance of cricket-loving Englishmen Charters and Caldicott, ably played by Basil Radford and Naunton Wayne, who first appeared in the film *The Lady Vanishes* and later in other movies, finally culminating in a TV series.

Film reviewer Richard Winnington wrote: 'A little more humour would not have been out of place, but as propaganda it proved an effective weapon. There is an unsentimental warm-heartedness which I hope we shall cling to, and extend, in filmed representations of the British scene.'

Eric later told a journalist that he had vivid impressions of the atmosphere created for this film, which included visits to large aircraft factories, and journeys in relays made by 'girl factory workers' to the London studios. A great many of the factory machines were also reproduced especially for the film. The journalist John Stapelton later commented on the scene where Eric's character picks up the petulant socialite (played by Anne Crawford) and dumps her unceremoniously in an air-raid shelter. He wrote: 'All over Britain, the girls thrilled to this, and Anne herself confessed to me that she had known worse moments. Here for the first time, Eric showed the masterful touch, and while some writhed in impotent fury, his feminine fan public increased.'

It must have come as something of a treat to Eric for being able to adopt a Yorkshire accent for the film, for not only was it his native accent, but he also grew to dislike the way that the majority of actors in British films were taught to speak in King's/Queen's English. A journalist wrote of him: 'He has never been one for following sheep-like in the fashion, whether it has been a new habit or picking up the latest and silliest slang. In fact, fashions in speech arouse him to instant Yorkshire scorn.'

Eric told him: 'I blame the acting schools for most of that 'refeened' stage talk we have to suffer in our theatres and cinemas. Accents of any sort should not be 'corrected'. Why should actors talk like gentlemen from the Foreign Office? Why should they all look like them, either? All actors look vaguely alike, especially the successful ones.' In his later essay on acting, Eric wrote: '...I would say, to those who wish to be film stars, that elocution classes are only useful if there is some defect to be corrected.'

Escape To Danger was another film released that year and Eric is given a starring role as Arthur Lawrence, a British schoolteacher working in Denmark who is caught up in the chaos when the Nazis invade the country. Like the Powell and Pressburger movies, this was also intended as a propaganda piece, and one reviewer described it as: '...adequate propaganda hokum.' Directed by Lance Comfort and Victor Hanbury, and co-starring Anne Dvorak, this is another rarely-seen movie – unavailable on either DVD or video, though thankfully it has not suffered the same fate as *Squadron Leader X*, and I believe there are copies available at the British Film Institute, in London.

By the time all these films were released, Eric was still continuing his stage work, and still playing the title role in *Uncle Harry*, now at the Duke of York's Theatre, in London. The play's successful run was one more example of how and why he eventually earned the nickname 'Long-Run Eric'.

If Eric was best remembered on stage for his parts in other long-running plays such as *Separate Tables*, *His Excellency* and *The Browning Version*, then the movie role he is most probably best remembered for was in the wartime classic, from the Powell and Pressburger partnership, *A Canterbury Tale*.

The story begins as three people arrive in a village in Southern England during the Second World War. They are Alison Smith, (played by Sheila Sim) who is due to start working on a farm as a 'Land Girl', Bob Johnson, an American GI (played by real-life soldier Sergeant John Sweet) and Peter Gibbs (Dennis Price), a British soldier, taking a few days leave before being posted abroad. As they walk through the village, Alison gets attacked by the 'Glue Man' – a mysterious figure who pours glue on the hair of local women who date American soldiers in the hours of darkness. So the three become intrigued and attempt to solve the mystery and discover the identity of the assailant. While doing so, they befriend Eric's character, the eccentric Thomas Colpeper, JP, (Eric Portman) an eccentric local historian, who they suspect is the Glueman.

A reviewer on a movie website encapsulates the film with his/her review: 'Refreshing: 1) a platonic relationship between three handsome men and one beautiful woman; 2) The most violent scene is where the troops burst out clapping the Sergeant who repaired the slide projector. 3) A basic plot premise so flimsy, and yet so captivating. A most profitable way of spending two hours.'

However, while this film is considered by some to be one of those quintessential British films, it was also meant to be a propaganda film and, in this respect, it falls far short. It was meant to encourage the allies to stick together and win the war, and yet one reviewer stated that it remained: 'A curious propaganda piece…quite what Powell and Pressburger thought they were up to is hard to fathom. To most people, the intentions of the filmmakers remained highly mysterious', adding that: '…the authorities showed some reluctance to encourage its export to our allies.'

However, despite its dubious quality as a propaganda movie, many people, including myself, simply enjoyed the film, and viewed it as a real one-off in British cinema.

In 1945, Eric starred in the film *Great Day* in which he played retired soldier, Captain John Ellis, a veteran of the First World War, who is painfully struggling to keep up appearances in a small village. The 'great day' of the title concerns the forthcoming visit of Eleanor Roosevelt, and the preparations of the village residents for this event, thus containing a variety of story strands and sub-plots. The main story, though, concerns Ellis who has been unable to adapt to civilian life after his military experience, and is forever sponging off his family and has since become a heavy drinker. Ellis' daughter Margaret, (Sheila Sim) is on the verge of entering into a wealthy but loveless marriage so she can rescue her mother (Flora Robson) from poverty, caused by her father's excesses.

In the original play by Leslie Storm, Ellis eventually drowns himself in a nearby pond, but the film ends on an upbeat note, allowing him to survive, with a chance to change his ways before the President's wife arrives in the village. Eric obviously knew that his character would be instantly disliked by the audience, but it took a confident and skilled actor to get the audience to care for him and he certainly achieves this. In a later interview, one journalist wrote that Eric delivered '…a masterful piece of acting that forced sympathy even while it excited contempt.' The actor commented that he remained 'really sorry for that fellow,' and the journalist observed: 'I could see that (Eric's) success is based on the fact that he truly lives the part he plays.'

Eric's next film was *Men of Two Worlds* (1946), set in remote and primitive Africa, cut off from modern society. Although he and Phyllis Calvert had supporting roles, they shared equal star-billing on the poster.

The plot concerns a famous African musician and composer, Kisenga, who has made a name for himself in Europe, before returning to his native country. The dreaded sleeping sickness, carried by the tsetse fly, is creeping near the village where Kisenga's people, the Litu, are living. Eric plays District Commissioner Randall, who wants to move the tribe to clearer land, away from the tsetse bush, but the Litu refuse to co-operate because they are under the influence of their witch doctor, Magole. Randall sends Kisenga to reason with his people. He is contemptuous of Magole and ancient superstition, and strives to show his people how progress and knowledge await them in the new land. After a quite intense psychological battle between the two men, Kisenga defeats Magole, winning the trust of his people and thus leads them to safer lands.

When Eric got cast in the role, Joyce Carey, who wrote the script, told him: 'You're the very image of the Commissioner I had in mind.' The film was unusual because it was the first British movie to hold its premier in Dar es Salaam, Tanganyika, in the East African territory. A report on 13th July 1946 (coincidentally, Eric's 45th birthday) read that a copy of the film "…left Britain by special plane this week and will probably be shown the following Monday. Sir William Battershill, Governor of Tanganyika, recorded a short speech which was incorporated into the film for its first night.'

A journalist described how the theatre had to take second place in Eric's career at this point, having committed to several new films, but said that '…those who saw his excellent stage performance as the English fascist in *Zero Hour*, in London last year, are aware that his tremendous acting talents are indeed as discernible on the stage as on the screen.'

The journalist commented on Eric's versatility as an actor, saying it was this which at least partly accounted for his success.

It pointed out how Eric was not merely aiming for stardom, for he was first and foremost an actor, having spent his life acting and he was determined to continue with it as long as the public wanted to see him. 'To frame the particular secret which lies behind his amazing popularity into an apt phrase would be difficult' nevertheless it would be safe to submit that one of the main reasons is that all his portrayals are 'excitingly different'.'

As Eric intimated several times over his career, he spent much time considering what films to make. He could quite easily have become a character actor, either choosing – or being persuaded by agent or film company – to specialise in playing one particular character type, such as a ruthless villain or bluff northerner, etc, but he was adamant that he would not be cajoled or pigeon-holed.

Eric told a journalist that he had no preference for what 'type' of character he liked to portray. He said: 'I'll play any type so long as I feel it's right for me. I like to experiment. That's why I don't appear in classical plays. Some actors feel they simply must tackle the great parts, but whilst there are certain ones – Othello, for instance – I would like to play myself, I'm of the opinion that they are performed too often as it is…I think that one or two of us should try to break fresh ground.'

In 1945, a press report stated that while Eric had appeared in various first-class pictures, his 'star status' had remained stationary rather than ascending the heights following the worldwide success of *The 49th Parallel*, and thus Eric had not 'acquired the significance' of Ronald Colman in *Random Harvest* or Robert Donat in *Mr Chips*. It argued that despite Eric's obvious acting ability, based on hard work including many years of theatrical experience, he was not on the same 'star' level as someone like David Niven or Edward G. Robinson, but possibly would have been by now if *The 49th Parallel* had been produced in America, and his subsequent career would have taken off from there instead. Having said that, this wasn't a 'dig' at Eric's career. Far from it. The writer pointed out that top-ranking British screen actors were '…not so plentiful in this country that we can allow them to chase bigger opportunities for worldwide acclaim in the States,' and that Eric would need the 'right kind' of stories to assure he is always ranked amongst the greats. 'That's what Portman needs. Opportunities in good pictures.'

As it happens, Eric's next film was one for which he would be remembered for many years to come and considered one of his very best. His first screen role as a killer came in 1946 in *Wanted For Murder*, a British crime film directed by Lawrence Huntington. He plays Victor James Colebrooke, the grandson of a notorious hangman, who is gradually becoming insane, and is the notorious strangler responsible for a string of murders across London. He is due to meet his friend Anne Fielding (played by Dulcie Gray). As Anne makes her way through the London Underground to meet Colebrooke, she meets a man called Jack Williams (Derek Farr) whose train has been delayed, and they take an instant liking to one another. He accompanies Anne to her meeting with Victor. Inspector Conway (played by Roland Culver) investigates the string of murders perpetrated by Victor and, as he gathers the evidence, he notices that much of it has been left behind, almost purposefully it seems, by Victor. Emeric Pressburger was also on the writing team, as he had been for Lance Comfort's *Squadron Leader X*, after winning awards for his previous work. In addition to the four leading stars, Stanley Holloway, who appeared in Eric's first film *The Girl from Maxims'*, featured in a supporting role as a police sergeant. Lynn Hudson wrote to tell me of how she appeared as an extra in the movie, and was one of a crowd of 'terrified onlookers' who watched Eric's character being chased by police across London's Hyde Park. It was later pointed out how Eric must have been in prime physical condition, because he performed twenty-five successive re-takes in an ice-cold tank for the drowning scene in the movie.

In a review, James Agee described it as: '...a pleasant and unpretentious thriller of the second or third grade.'

In 1946, Eric also made the movie *Daybreak*, but due to some trouble with the BBFC (British Board of Film Censors) it was not released until 1948. Directed by Compton Bennett, it is described as 'film noir drama'. With a strange twist to the lead character in his previous film *Wanted For Murder*, where he played the grandson of a hangman, here he actually plays the hangman himself, who is called to England's prisons to perform executions. Needless to say he doesn't broadcast the fact and his 'day job' is a barber. The only other person who knows his secret vocation, is his assistant Ron (played by Bill Owen, who would later find fame as Compo in the BBC TV series *The Last of the Summer Wine*).

He meets a woman called Frankie (played by Ann Todd) and they get married, and soon after Eddie's father dies, leaving him the family barge business working on the River Thames. So Eddie passes the barber shop to Ron, while he and Frankie move onto one of the barges. He hires a Scandinavian seaman, Olaf, (played by Maxwell Reed), and after Eddie catches him and Frankie having an affair, the two men get into a fight. Eddie falls overboard and fails to resurface, and then Olaf gets arrested for murder as it is assumed Eddie is dead and his body carried out to sea. In despair, Frankie commits suicide, but Eddie has managed to swim ashore and take refuge with Ron.

When Olaf is sentenced to execution, guess who gets called to perform it? Eddie, the hangman, is appointed to do the dirty deed, but he cannot go through with it and confesses to the authorities who he is. He returns to the barber's shop and prepares to end his own life.

Eric's next film was another crime thriller called *Dear Murderer*, directed by fellow Yorkshireman Arthur Crabtree, of Shipley, Bradford, who had served as cinematographer on the actor's earlier film *Uncensored* (1942).

Eric plays Lee Warren, who is pathologically jealous of his wife Vivien (played by Greta Gynt) who is devious and habitually unfaithful and who despises him.

When Lee returns from a business trip, he finds several cards addressed to Vivien, with the words 'Love Always' and determines to kill her latest lover Richard Fenton (played by Dennis Price).

He does kill Fenton, but not before persuading him to write a letter to Vivien ending the relationship. As the letter looks like a suicide note, Lee believes he has committed the perfect crime, and that the police will believe Fenton committed suicide.

However, it soon transpires that Fenton had simply been humouring Lee by writing the letter, as he and Vivien had ended the relationship some time before. Guilt-stricken at having murdered Fenton, Lee is also quick to realise that the police will question whether or not Fenton had committed suicide.

When he learns that Vivien has taken a new lover Jimmy Martin (played by Maxwell Reed, who also played opposite him in *Daybreak*), he sees a chance to extricate himself and getting him away from Vivien at the same time, so he frames Martin for Fenton's murder. While it looks like the plan has worked, Inspector Pembury (played by Jack Warner who would later return to the police for the title role in TV series *Dixon of Dock Green*), has his doubts and suspects Lee is behind it, but is unable to prove the man's guilt. There are so many twists and turns in this movie, and it is thoroughly recommended.

Halliwell's described the film as a '...thoroughly artificial pattern play set among the unreal rich, from one of those unaccountable West End successes, here boringly filmed.' Although Alan Dent, in *News Chronicle*, thought it: 'A quite alarming picture.'

Eric's next film was *The Mark of Cain*, where he played one of two brothers who become infatuated with a young woman, played by Sally Gray, and Eric plays the villainous one. Directed by Brian Desmond. Halliwell's describes the movie as a 'Turgid melodrama with many opportunities offered and none taken.'

I can't find any record of Eric performing in a play in Belfast, so perhaps he was here on holiday or a social visit when J. W. Connolly met him in 1946.

Mr Connolly tells me: '(Eric) was staying in the Belgravia Hotel on the Lisburn Road. I started work there as an apprentice landscape gardener, and I also lived there, as my home was about ninety miles away. Some of the time, I would help out at night, cleaning the shoes that guests left outside the doors, and so I shined his shoes at the time. In 1947, I travelled to Manchester and worked at the Queen's Hotel in Piccadilly for a time. One day, I was walking away from the hotel, when I heard a voice behind me saying 'What are *you* doing here?' It was Eric Portman and he had recognised me from Belfast. After a little talk, he wished me well. I thanked him, but never saw him again. I was told he used to go for a drink at the Lord Nelson pub on Oldham Street in Manchester. He was always very polite and had a distinctive voice and accent.'

That same year, Mrs B. Jackson saw the actor in North Yorkshire on 19th September 1946, and kindly sent me a signed photo of the actor. She says: 'My mother, sister and myself were on holiday in Scarborough, complete with our ration books! We were great film fans in those days when it was nearly the only visual entertainment. This photo was given out during an appearance by Eric Portman at the Open Air Theatre, during the

'Scarborough Welcome Home Week'. It was a welcome home for armed forces who had fought in the war. Most towns did it. I can't remember why Eric Portman was there, but a star would always draw the crowds.'

As most towns did indeed hold a Welcome Home Week, why did Eric choose Scarborough in particular? Christine Holliday may provide the answer. She told me: 'Although I was only a child of eight when the war finished, I remember (Eric Portman) visiting Scarborough, as frequently as travelling in those days would allow. He had an Aunt – whose name I have long since forgotten – who lived almost opposite us in Garfield Road. He must have arrived by train because apparently he would sell his autograph outside the station, with profits going to the warship funds. My mother used to say: "He's here again," and he would walk up the road, smartly dressed in a grey suit, with his raincoat slung over his shoulders, very much the actor. Nobody mobbed this matinee idol in our quiet neighbourhood – he simply visited his auntie and departed again, like a good nephew should!'

CHAPTER 4

PALS AT PENPOL

It is not clear when and where Eric Portman met the man who was to become his partner for the rest of his life. The only references to Knox Laing (pronounced Lang) I have ever found relate to four films and a stage play. He served as joint stage manager in the New York production of Terence Rattigan's play *French Without Tears*, where it ran on Broadway between 28th September 1937 and 1st January 1938. Therefore, Eric and Knox may have met through Rattigan or one of his friends or colleagues. Knox also served as Assistant Director to Lance Comfort on the film *Hotel Reserve* (1944), starring James Mason and Herbert Lom, and again to Jeffrey Dell on the movie *Don't Take it To Heart* (1944), starring Richard Greene. So maybe they met through Lance Comfort, as Eric was in three of the director's movies including *Squadron Leader X*. They may also have met through their mutual association with the company Box Films, in which Knox served as Production Manager on two movies produced by Sydney Box, including *The Seventh Veil* (1945), starring James Mason, Ann Todd and Herbert Lom and *29 Acacia Avenue* (1945) starring Gordon Harker.

There appeared to be some confusion on a movie website, when someone suggested Knox Laing was a pseudonym of the actor Harold

89

Lang who appeared with Eric in a few films, most notably *Cairo Road*. To add to the confusion, there was another famous Harold Lang, a dancer who also appeared in a few films, and there is a website dedicated to his life and career. But, as far as I know, there was no connection between Knox Laing and either of the two Harold Langs. The moral here, of course, is don't believe everything you read – particularly on the internet!

Eric's partner Knox Laing
(Courtesy of Mike Ferguson)

One of Eric and Knox's neighbours, John Ferguson, told me: 'No-one really knew much about Knox. He came from quite a wealthy family, but they disowned him when they discovered his homosexuality.'

John's son, Mike Ferguson, sent me the only known surviving photograph of Knox, and the only other information I have been able to discover was that he was born in Bedford and the fullest version of his name I could find was Knox Claude K. Laing.

The first mention of Eric and Knox I received after my appeal, was from two ladies who lived in the area where Eric bought a cottage.

Daphne Crawshaw told me: 'My mother Mary Esther Brooks was warwidowed at the age of thirty, when I was eight years old. My grandparents were retiring in 1946 from The Earl of Chatham, a little country inn at Lostwithiel, in Cornwall, and my mother applied to the brewery to take over from them as landlady, which she did. Sometime later, I do not know which year, she was serving in the bar one early evening, when two extremely handsome and cultured gentlemen came in for a round of drinks. The men – called Eric and Knox – said they were lost and looking for Penpol Cottage (which Eric wanted to buy) in the hamlet of Penpol, situated in the parish of St Veep. My mother was born in the cottage – with her six brothers and sisters, so she was able to give them directions.'

'From that day, whenever Eric and Knox went to Penpol from London, they always called on my mother at the pub. Seven years later, she remarried the landlord of the *King of Prussia*, in the Cornish town of Fowey (pronounced 'Foy'), and became Esther Harvey. Shortly afterwards, she was widowed again. The hotel was a large inn on the town quay with two bars, twelve letting bedrooms and fourteen staff. My father's sister – my Aunty May – came to Fowey every summer to help my Mother run the hotel. Every summer, Eric Portman would send his beautiful river launch from Penpol to Fowey to collect my Mother and Aunty to take them back to his house for dinner. Sadly, I was not included! Eric had renamed the cottage 'Penpol House' and my mother said it was magnificent. She also told me that Eric and Knox always had one or two beautiful young men staying with them. They were well-spoken, educated and cultured – but above all, they were charming and very good-looking!

Eric's cottage at Penpol

These young men covered the duties of cook, waiter, valet, butler and housekeeper – but always joined them at the dinner table. At the end of these memorable evenings, the tide was invariably too low to return to Fowey by launch, so one of the young men would be detailed to return my

Mother and Aunt to Fowey by car – and these cars would be top-of-the-range. Homosexuality was, at the time, illegal, but my mother was broad-minded and the criteria she used was how anyone treated her. Both Eric and Knox treated these two middle-aged ladies with great charm and respect and my mother was very fond of them. When my Aunt returned to her home in Kent after each summer, she would tell her friends that she had dined with Eric Portman and his partner – but no-one ever believed her!'

'When I was a very little girl, Eric Portman wrote a message for me in my Autograph Book and I still remember what he wrote:

Daphne –
to the beloved child, may she grow in her graces
and be blessed in all her walks in life –
My *salannas to her,
Eric Portman
(* salannas is an Eastern greeting)

Another lady who got to know Eric was Doris Vincent, who told me: 'I remember him very well. My parents ran the King of Prussia Hotel in Fowey, Cornwall. Although during the war, it was called The King's Hotel, as you can no doubt understand why. So it was the King's Hotel when Eric Portman was here, and Eric and his friends were regular guests.'

'His regular guest was Knox Laing and, occasionally, Elsie and Doris Waters (who appeared in films and who also had a radio show) amongst many others. He brought a lot of famous people (from films) down to his cottage. He would visit Fowey by car from Penpol, though sometimes he would come down by motor boat.'

'Knox Laing was his producer/manager, though Eric later called him his housekeeper. I used to go dancing with Eric and others to St Austell Public Rooms and Fowey Town Hall. I remember he was a great dancer. I also have an autograph from him signed in 1946. He was a delightful person and I have happy memories of him in my home. Eric was a lovely gentleman. A quiet person and a delight to know.'

Eric at home in Penpol

Mavis Johns kindly sent me a photograph of Eric Portman's cottage at Penpol taken in 1948, saying: 'I used to live very near to Penpol in the parish of St Veep. I never met him, but often saw him around Fowey with his friends.'

Christine Broom told me: 'My father was born in 1920 at Mill Farm, at Penpol. This was opposite the cottage where Eric Portman lived from the 1940s. One of my father's sisters, Mabel Whetter, was housekeeper for many years to Eric Portman and his companion Knox Laing. She went to the cottage each morning from ten until midday, and again from four until five in the afternoon, and then returned from nine until ten in the evening, which she did seven days a week, though I don't think her remuneration was good!'

'I remember them very well and I was always pleased to see them when I visited my grandparents, aunts and uncles each Autumn. I recall Eric Portman impeccably dressed in a silk dressing gown with a white silk scarf around his neck. Knox Laing had been a film producer and he stayed at the cottage when Eric was away filming. He always seemed to wear leather sandals! They kept dogs and bred bull terriers and I remember one white puppy named Claude which they sold to someone in Paris.'

'I seem to remember Knox was a smoker and they both liked alcohol. I think they had a sports car which Knox drove but I also seem to remember he had a serious accident at one time.'

John and Barbara Ferguson also knew Eric, Knox and Mabel Whetter. Mr Ferguson recalls: 'The Whetter family were Mabel, Emily and Henry, who all knew Eric when he lived at Penpol. Mabel would clean, and look after, the inside of the cottage. Emily would walk two miles into Fowey to do their shopping. Henry would take care of Eric's garden. Instead of wages, he would get all the apples in the field at the back of the house. Eric had about twenty-four apple trees, and Henry would make cider from them which lasted him a year. When Eric and Knox went away, we would stay in the cottage and would always invite the Whetters over for a drink with us.'

Eric's home at Penpol

Mr Ferguson sent me some photos of Eric's cottage and garden, and the get-togethers which he and his wife had with the Whetter family, while Eric and Knox were away from home.

In the book *Film Stars At Home: 1946-1947* (1947), the author (name unknown) recounts being invited to the actor's home, and writes:

'This bachelor star realised a long-standing ambition when he bought a 200-year-old cottage in Cornwall recently, and set about turning it into his ideal home. The old cottage nestles at the foot of the uplands which comprise the farm he acquired at the same time, and there was a great deal (which) had to be done to it. One of the first improvements he effected was to substitute manger doors made of chestnut wood for the original ones. He points out that these keep out wind and rain without shutting out the lovely view of the rolling hills and fields. He also removed the small cottage windows and built in long low ones that let the maximum light into the rooms. Most of the work of converting and reconditioning he has done single-handed, under the watchful eyes of his companion, Lofty, half-collie, half-something else; Gay, the young water spaniel, and his two cats, Gypsy and Tiz.'

'Eric does all his own cooking on the Aga stove – the one modern concession he has installed in his ancient Cornish home. Even the water has to be drawn from a natural spring – he doesn't believe in house-keeping the easy way. He has laid out a delightful unconventional flower garden round the cottage and planted an orchard. In his pleasant sitting room, huge logs burn in the lovely old grate, built from Cornish slate and stone. There couldn't be a better spot to relax between long sessions at the studio.'

A journalist would later write that Eric's '... spare time is divided between London and Cornwall. A dwarf cottage with a roof-garden off Sloane Square is where the actor's friends meet him in town. He seldom dines out, especially when he's working at studio or theatre. If he does, it's always a quiet get-

95

together with two or three cronies at popular meeting places for people in show business. Eric could never be described as a 'night clubber'. The expensive establishments around Piccadilly, hardly see him at all. His heart, he says, has been house-trained, for a two-storey cottage with seven rooms near Fowey on the south-west coast. It is two hundred years old and he has furnished it with antiques and other valuables bought at auctions or tracked down by traders all over the world. Here, there's a lovely terrace where, each summer, weekend guests toast their eyes on a tranquil view, or wander in the ten-acre gardens or the smallholding where there are fowls and a pig. He walks to the local inn, two miles, with his chauffeur-companion, Harry, a former Desert Rat, and his bull terriers, Susan and Toffy, and Gay, the spaniel. He also has the reputation of throwing a nifty dart – "For a left-hander," says one purist.'

Eric at home with his beloved pets (source unknown)

Eric spent much time in Fowey and Tim Raymond told me: 'My parents ran the Marina Hotel, in Fowey, and I met Eric a couple of times when he came to dine there with his friend Jack Vickers. Jack ran a local restaurant and was also the Mayor of Fowey. As I was only briefly introduced to (Eric), we never had much time to chat!'

In 1950, Eric agreed to write an article for the *Fowey Magazine*, with the front cover proclaiming the town as 'The Centre of the Cornish Riviera'.

In the article entitled 'What Fowey Means To Me', he wrote: 'I remember when I first went to Fowey. I was fairly young and quite hard up, so I had no silly ideas then – no more than I have now – of staying in large fashionable places 'costing the earth.' I was fascinated at once by the lovely simplicity of Cornwall. I was able to wear really easy country clothes (nobody cares what you wear in Cornwall, so everybody has that casual interesting individuality – so delightful after stuffy orthodox town-life). My first view of Fowey was on a summer's evening when the little lights on the boats were beginning to show on the wide serene river. How thrilling it was; with a beauty so romantic and in a way so touching that I could not get the feeling of Cornwall out of my mind. I never did. Some years afterwards, I decided to buy a little house on an estuary between Fowey and Lerryn. All my most enchanting days have been spent there. There is a quality about Fowey and its river and the brilliant purple-blue of the sea beyond – quite unlike the blue of any sea anywhere else in the world

Eric's article for the *Fowey Magazine*

– which has the power to calm tired nerves and all unhappiness. One feels safe there: and when one has to be in London "on the job", I think of Cornwall – for me specially of Fowey – and long to be there again: in two words I would call it "Another World".'

Eric later told a journalist that being at his home in Cornwall, away from the movie set, coupled with doing a job he loved, was his own definition of success.

He said: 'Being successful is being able to admire the reflection of the fire in your own Chippendale bookcase or being able to laze in your own comfortable chair, with your pets snoozing on the rug before the welcome blaze. And in summer, for me, it means as many hours as I can snatch on my cottage-cum-farm, which my success enabled me to buy last year in Cornwall. These blessings result from earning my own money in a job that I enjoy. It makes me desperately unhappy to see thousands of people doing work they dislike all the days of their lives. One is thankful one has made a go of the job of acting.'

Eric and one of his pet dogs (source unknown)

CHAPTER 5

ACTING UP

On one of his trips home in September 1947, Eric gave a speech to the Business and Professional Women's Club. The club's report of the occasion read: 'Eric Portman's contention that women are the most important section of the film-going public was certainly borne out by the record attendance of members at this week's meeting … And further support of the claim was shown in the presence of a contingent of our daughter club, Batley and Dewsbury, who had chosen for their last visit, Mr Portman's lecture from the last syllabus, which this year shows a very promising list of speakers. The lecture was discursive, amusing and conducted in an informal conversational style which was very easy on the large number of feminine ears which had brought along to hear this well-known personality of the stage and screen, who was known as a child to many of his audience. Mr Portman said there is a great demand for murder films, and mentioned that in film-making an important job always allotted to a woman is ensuring complete continuity of the details of hair and dress and accessories of the characters in the various scenes. It is easy to realise the importance of such vigilance. In answer to a question about the dearth of women film directors, Mr Portman said there were two very good ones, Mary Field and Muriel Box, but could offer no suggestions as to why their ranks remained so thin.

It was perhaps comforting for the hard-working Yorkshire audience to hear from an authentic source that many of the well-known Hollywood stars are not nearly as glamorous in real life as on the screen. Miss G. Haslem, who taught the small boy Eric Portman, many years ago, proposed a very enthusiastic vote of thanks.'

That same month, Eric signed a new contract with the J. Arthur Rank Organization to make six films in the next six years, and while still on the subject of acting, there is a line attributed to Eric Portman, which I have failed to source.

The quote is: 'Acting is like masturbation. You either do it, or don't do it – but you never talk about it!'

A signed photograph for fans (source unknown)

Where and when and why he said it, must remain a mystery, though I suspect it was simply meant to be a private comment to someone rather than a comment intended for public consumption.

As already stated, Eric wrote an essay on film acting, which was included in a book on the subject (see bibliography). He wrote: 'A great many people dream of a star's success on the films. It's a good dream, for it answers the requirements of most of the wishes (which) most of us want to have fulfilled.

The screen star does get rewarded – money and fame are not small figures in the sum total of ambition. But I want to talk to those who are quite determined to turn the dream into reality, and who realise that such a transformation does require a terrific amount of determination.'

'Now, most people might imagine that one of the greatest difficulties for the film actor is caused by the fact that a film is shot in a number of short scenes.'

'Let us examine what actually happens. The actor is called on the set. He has to be ready for the time he is called, but this does not mean that everyone else will be ready for him. The actor may arrive on the set in just the mood to play his scene. But the cameraman is probably having trouble with a little model which is being placed in position in front of the camera – on the screen the model will blend with the set and give the impression that the company has built the whole inside of a cathedral instead of just two pillars and a scrap of floor, or the scene artist is still busy painting in some trick perspective on the back-cloth. Whatever is going on, it probably is some form of delay for the actor. He has to wait and, probably, during the delay, he loses his good mood. Then, suddenly, he realises that the director is calling for him. One moment he is thinking, perhaps, of nothing in particular, and the next he has to plunge into the heart of a special scene. It is as if the actor had to turn on his art like an electric lamp. And when the little scene is over, the actor has to wait once more. The lamp turned out. Yet the film actor has to be ready to switch it on again for the next scene – just when the order comes.'

'I would (say that the film actor's greatest difficulty) is the enormous amount of *concentration* which is needed to play a film scene. There is the necessity of remembering the action exactly. You must undo your coat at precisely one minute, pick up your briefcase at precisely another, etc. The scene is planned for full consideration for the microphone and camera, to happen one way and that is the way it must happen. On stage, a good actor can get away with murder. If he forgets to pick-up the briefcase on the right line, he can go back for it. A good stage actor can always catch up with himself again. But if a screen-actor forgets his brief-case at the right moment, and if he attempts to go back for it, he will probably find that he is now cutting between another artiste and the lens, or interfering with some intricate camera movement.'

'It has often struck me that women seem to be able to learn action-concentration for film work more easily than men. In studios, the person who checks on and records the little details of routine is always a *continuity girl*. 'No, Mr X,' says the continuity writer without looking at her notes, 'in the last scene you put the glass just here, and the siphon just there.' But in films, whether it is a question of female star or male star, the function must be one hundred per cent concentration for the action – and the words.'

'On the stage, an actor can be prompted, and the audience need never know that the actor has forgotten his lines. There can be no prompter during a film-take.'

'I would like you to think of a film scene as a sort of burning glass of concentration. I'm not exaggerating. You must remember that a film appears on the screen magnified to over life-size. In a close-up, the magnification may be forty times that of the living face. It is possible for a stage actor to think of other things while he says his lines. Especially if he is in the middle of a long run, a stage actor can plan in his mind his dinner at 'The Ivy', while he talks to the heroine about the hunger of love. If he is a skilled actor, the audience need never lose conviction that the actor means what he is saying. But with the film actor, the merest flicker of inattention registers. All the actor's thoughts must be concentrated for the burning glass of the film scene.'

'…it isn't necessary to be good-looking to be a film star. The thing you do need, if you want a career in lights and not just a meteor-flash, is the ability to arrest an audience.'

'It's hard to analyse this ability. It comes, I suppose, in part from sex motifs, and in part from the concentration, the professional touch of certainty, which the good actor gives to his performance. It isn't looks. It isn't the articulation of the voice, although the quality of the voice may have something to do with it. You can see a film in a foreign language, a language you do not understand, and yet be held by the performance of some of the actors. It isn't looks. It isn't the voice. It's personality.'

'I'm afraid that word has brought us back to where we started this attempt at analysis. Philosophers, biologists and psychoanalysts have all tried to define personality; but they haven't really been able to give us a workable formula of words. Perhaps the best definition is the old theatrical one of audience-projection. The actor with personality projects his inner force, he makes it leap across the footlights or from the screen. There is an actual psychic contact between the player and the spectator. It's a wonder, for those who have it, and a mystery.'

'In a rough way, I would say you can test your audience-projection in ordinary life. The next time you go into a crowded room, see if you can project your personality. See if people stop talking when you enter, look at you, rise quickly to give you a seat, a drink, a cigarette. But if we try to take the question of personality any further, we will land in mysticism. All I can say, in summing up, is that you should know if you've got personality, from the reactions of your friends – and enemies.'

'So, personality can make you a film star. Whether you are a film actor or not, will depend on your histrionic talent. Obviously, you must have some little talent for acting, if you are to avoid the fake class.'

'My advice, then, to any young man or woman who wants to become a film star is – learn your business on stage. Develop your acting talents. And the stage will also give you the self-assurance you need to face the camera and microphone. Believe me, it can be a terrifying encounter.'

'Yes, I did start myself on the stage. I have not been cheating! I worked for years in *little theatres*. Working in little art-theatres is a great help to the film actor who has to pose in front of a piece of back-projection (a background scene on which a film is projected) and pretend that he is in some far-off country. Little art-theatres teach one to stand in front of anything and pretend one is anywhere. From the little theatres, I moved to the West End. Anyone who is doubtful about my advice to start on the stage, should remember that film companies are always sending their talent scouts to the theatre. Many directors make a habit of going to plays in search of new blood for the studios.'

'I know there are people who, because they are not interested in the stage as a career, think that their first move towards film stardom ought to be by way of crowd work in the film studios. Personally, I think this is a great mistake. Crowd work is an art of its own. You have to move in the crowd with the crowd. You have to learn to make yourself a background. The crowd artiste who is individual is a bad crowd artiste. The would-be star, who tries to get experience by way of the crowd, will be learning too many wrong lessons. He, or she, will be learning how to pass practically unnoticed by an audience. But the star – must arrest the audience's attention.'

'Without doubt, there have been exceptions: some crowd artistes have become stars. But I recommend stage training. Better to have a few weeks as a stand-in rather than years of 'extra' work, if you want to get the feel of the studio and end up a top liner.'

'The stand-in is the man, or woman, who stands in the set in the position which will be occupied by the star, while the camera-man arranges his lights. But the stage-trained actor will hardly need stand-in experience. Part of his stage training will have been self-assurance...'

'...Film actors are very well treated in the studio. But, like all film workers, they have to work hard. The hours are generally from eight in the morning to seven at night. Six months of a film probably corresponds to about three years' run of a play in working hours. If I were a mathematician, I would try and give you it in terms of extra matinees.'

'So we come to the fact that cannot be shirked – the film star works. The gold is there, it glitters under the arc lights, but – the film star has to earn it.'

Up to this point, Eric's major movie work was for the established film companies, and yet his next choice was to digress from this. The film *Corridor of Mirrors* sees him playing Paul Mangin, a man obsessed by the belief that he is the reincarnation of the lover of a girl, Venetia, in a four-hundred-year-old Italian painting. When he meets Mifanwy Conway, (portrayed by Edana Romney) he is convinced she is the reincarnation of Venetia. She comes under his spell and he delights in seeing her dressed in the period costumes he keeps in mirrored cupboards in a corridor in his beautiful home.

The film was different to previous work, because it was considered an 'art-house' project, rather than a 'commercial' film, co-written and co-produced by its star, Edana Romney. An aspiring film actress, constantly rejected for acting roles, the story of how she came to make the movie is a fascinating one; a story of determination and passion – and no doubt one that won the respect of Eric Portman.

Edana came to London from Johannesburg in 1937 and was accepted by drama school RADA (Royal Academy of Dramatic Art), by upping her age. She won a few prizes for her performances, and yet theatrical agents wouldn't take her on. Non-photogenic. No screen personality. No sex appeal, they claimed. So she embarked on a do-it-yourself career, by deciding: '…there was only one thing I could do, and that was to write myself into films. I would write something which the film industry would want enough to have me along with it!'

Edana met Rudolph Cartier, an unknown Viennese scriptwriter working in England. They found they had similar ideas and formed a 'highly-theoretical' company called Apollo Films. A man called Mr Gottlieb agreed to finance them – if they showed him a signed distribution contract, a script and an option on a studio. So they wrote the script of *Corridor of Mirrors*, based on a novel by Christopher Massey. Rank Films liked it and promised distribution if they could get a star to play opposite Edana. She persuaded some financiers to back the film but had to wait for studio space at places like Denham and Pinewood, competing with more established companies, and was told that there wouldn't be any studio space for them for another three years. After all that time, they were offered the chance to be the first British company to film in France.

Edana said: 'It was a studio called Buttes-Chaumont and it was supposed to be the oldest film studio in the world. We found it so old that when we put up the camera crane on one of the floors it fell through the rotting boards. But there was a feeling of adventure about the whole thing.'

Says Edana: 'They have a system there of working right through without a break from 12pm to 7pm and due to the co-operative spirit of everyone in the unit, we were able to finish shooting and not overboard on the cost.'

Big movie companies told them the film could not be made successfully, but – like all great pioneers – they ignored the dissenters and backstabbers and pushed ahead with production regardless. Luckily, the film's director was multi-talented and could speak French. The day the shooting began, they all breathed a heavy sigh of relief having overcome all the obstacles. By an unhappy quirk, the film's financier Mr Gottlieb was killed on the same day in a car crash, but such was his faith in the project, he had already pledged his fortune to them in advance, so the filming could begin.

The sum of £600 was invested in a test of Edana, to persuade a star to act with an unknown in a film made by unknowns, including screenwriter Terence Young, who aspired to be a film director.

Edana said: 'I think the picture will prove he has a very fine future, and he did so much to help me and all the cast by his sensitive, imaginative directing.' Terence Young did indeed prove to have a fine future and he has directed many famous movies including three in the James Bond franchise: *Dr No*, *From Russia with Love* and *Thunderball*.

A journalist later wrote of how Eric came to be involved in the film: 'Perhaps this anxiety to help others, and a determination to go through with it in true Yorkshire fashion, helped to influence his decision to play the part of the psychopathic romantic lead in *Corridor of Mirrors*, which has given a large number of actors and technicians their first chance in pictures. They had hardly dared hope Eric Portman, an established star, would like the part and, even more, agree to play it.'

A magazine reported that Eric was first choice to play the role, and told how he '…seized the chance to help them, threw up offers right and left, and saved the careers of a handful of courageous people.'

Edana commented: 'I'm eternally grateful to Eric Portman for having the courage to play with an unknown girl with an unknown company. I think it was very great of him.'

Despite the state of the tiny ill-equipped Parisian studio, including rotting floorboards and the bitter cold (Eric had to suck ice-cubes to prevent his breath from clouding) it was a very happy unit and the French technicians got infected with Edana's enthusiasm and worked with a willingness that did much to mitigate the difficulties.

Eric went to the Chamber of Horrors at Madame Tussaud's on the evening of *Friday 13th* December, to have his effigy made for use in one of the scenes. When he got there, he heard loud cries and shouts for help and someone banging on the door. So he followed the direction of the shouts and found the owner, Mr Tussaud, had been locked in his own Chamber of Horrors by a careless nightwatchman!

Described by a journalist as an 'unusually beautiful drama of a man who is obsessed by the past and lives for beauty and the woman who falls under

Eric Portman at the premiere of *Corridor of Mirrors*, with co-star and co-producer Edana Romney at his side and Queen Mary (wife of King George V) on the extreme right (source unknown)

the spell of his strange fascination, then fights to free herself from it. The elegance and richness of the settings, the mobility and beauty of the camera work are alone worth seeing. Eric Portman dominates the film with his sensitive portrayal of its strange hero, and newcomer Edana Romney is photographed magnificently.'

Although there were some negative reviews of the film. One described it as a '…pretentious melodrama of no urgent narrative interest, with all concerned sadly at sea.' Another wrote: 'It has aimed at Art. It is, in fact, Effect. Some members of the cast wander in and out of the scenes as if they are not quite sure what has happened to them. Their confusion is not beyond comprehension.'

The celebrated actor, Sir Christopher Lee, CBE, who is probably best remembered for portraying Count Dracula in the Hammer Horror films, well remembers a scene in the film, as it was the first in which he ever spoke on screen. He told Tony Earnshaw: 'I was with a group of people – Hugh Latimer, John Penrose, Mavis Villiers, Lois Maxwell, and the star of the film, Edana Romney – sitting at a table in a nightclub. Eric appeared in the door and I said: 'Look, standing in the entrance, Lord Byron.' Eric Portman was a big name in the British film industry. I was a nobody. I didn't know him, I barely spoke to him, and I never had scenes with him. That's 65 years ago but you never forget your first line in a film. And that was my solitary communication with Eric Portman.'

In August 1947, Eric was interviewed by John Stapelton and the journalist wrote: 'My first impression of Eric Portman was his charming smile as he walked towards me across the studio floor. This is not say that he smiles less or more so than most folk, but it is a side of his nature that has not often been seen on the screen, for Eric is fast gaining a reputation as the actor who plays unusual parts.'

'Two of his successive leading ladies, themselves both stars of the first rank, spontaneously said…'Oh, Eric Portman, the nicest leading man I know.' From all quarters, I was told of his unfailing quiet courtesy and how working with him was to feel that one's best was somehow brought to the surface and given an extra polish.'

'Then came *Wanted for Murder* which many have voted his finest film to date (August 1947). There was a dual personality and the pathetic struggle against the dark forces of libide so accurately expressed. Although he played a stranger and a madman, such finesse was put into the part that created sympathy, for Eric realises that no villain is entirely bad, and he knows that the secret of such portraits lies in the delicate shades and not in the liberal application of stark black.'

Stapelton suggested that a film based on the recent tragedy of the sadist Heath (*Neville Heath was executed in 1946 for the murders of two young women) would give him fine scope, and Eric agreed that with 'suitable modifications it might make a fine picture and sound a psychological warning.'

Eric had a knack for choosing to star in stage plays which were then made into movies, but is this so surprising, for he always searched for a production with a strong and interesting character to portray, which could often be translated from stage to screen, without losing any of its quality. One such example was *The Blind Goddess*, released in 1948, and based on the stage play by Patrick Hastings.

It is a British drama directed by Harold French, where a secretary sets out to expose his boss, Lord Brasted, for embezzlement and Eric played the solicitor who handles the case.

It re-teamed the actor with his *Millions Like Us* co-star Anne Crawford, and the cast also included Michael Denison, Claire Bloom, Maurice Denham, and with Hugh Williams as Lord Brasted.

Gordon Musgrove, a journalist for the magazine *Film Illustrated Monthly*, was invited along to Gainsorough Studios in Islington and watch the filming of *The Blind Goddess*. On arrival, Musgrove had to wait at the door in the front office, on which there was a red light, indicating that the crew were filming a scene. When the red light switched off, the journalist was ushered into the studio. Soon afterwards, the red light was switched back on again and everyone was told to be quiet, as the cameras started rolling.

This was a scene between Eric Portman and Anne Crawford, and Musgrove stood motionless some feet away from the camera. For this take, the camera was on Eric, and the same scene would be shot again later with camera pointing at Anne. He was told that the two shots would be combined and edited together later. After the scene was shot, Eric and Anne came off-set to have their make-up retouched, and the director, Harold French, explained to his team what he wanted them to do in preparation for the next scene when, wrote Musgrove, there were '..dozens of people all doing their jobs with quiet precision.'

After the next scene had been filmed, Musgrove went to the local ale house for a drink with Eric. He wrote: 'To be with Eric off the set is a wonderful experience. A cheery word to all, and everyone knows and senses his friendliness. Mine host at the local did us proud and Eric once more enhanced his popularity by chatting with the 'locals' and buying them a drink.'

Eric told him what he planned to do after work on the film was completed. 'I'd like a rest at my little cottage, but I doubt if I shall get that. You see, I start my new (film) contract on March 1st and really don't know what they have in mind for me. I know they are interested in Walpole's *The Killer and The Slain* and I have always wanted to play it. I hope it will be my next film'. (*This was later cancelled by the production company for being 'too morbid.')

In the afternoon, Harold French allowed Musgrove to accompany Eric, Anne and the rest of the team into the adjoining theatre to see the 'rushes'. 'This was a great privilege and rarely allowed, so we felt duly honoured,' wrote the journalist. In his essay on acting, Eric discusses this process. He writes: 'At the end of the studio day, the actor is always welcomed by the production staff at the showing of the rushes – the first prints of the previous day's takes. This co-operation on the part of the production staff is an enormous help to the actor. While the stage actor has to wait till the first night before he can tell how his characterisation has succeeded, the film actor can follow the rushes. If he is quite honest with himself, he can see where his style needs a change for the role he is playing.'

The group the returned to the studios to shoot the same scenes again, but this time with the camera pointing at Anne Crawford. The journalist commented that she acted so convincingly that after one of the takes, everyone applauded. Another scene required what the journalist called 'quite clever camera work, necessitating quick movement on the 'dolly'. During one of the takes cameraman Dudley Lovell's pathetic "I'm sorry, I can't go on any longer," brought a round of laughter.'

On another occasion, the 'clapper boy' caught one of the lights with his head and moved it, and this meant starting again. Musgrove wrote: 'Once more, Eric proved what a grand person he is, by remarking: "That's his first mistake. He sets us a good example." This (comment) did much to remove the lad's embarrassment.'

The film *Daybreak*, (already featured), was released in 1948, creating the illusion that Eric had made three films in quick succession, but in fact, it was shot in 1946, and its release was delayed due to various unknown issues with the BBFC (British Board of Film Censors).

CHAPTER 6

THE RATTIGAN CONNECTION

'After eight years making movies, Eric Portman has made the most triumphant return to the theatre,' declared a journalist in September 1948. 'His acting as the middle-aged schoolmaster in Rattigan's *The Browning Version* at the Phoenix Theatre, is one of the most brilliant performances in modern theatre. For many years, Portman has been one of the most considerable screen actors we possess, and theatregoers with longer memories will recall his magnificent performances as Byron and Brutus in pre-war years.'

Eric said: 'Years in films have definitely helped my stage work. I disagree with those actors who say that the two worlds are so totally different that one has no influence on the other. I have definitely profited through my years of concentrated close-up work in the film studios. It has helped me to project across the footlights the mental processes of the disillusioned schoolmaster and in every way I feel that screen technique puts a final polish upon one's stage work.'

Despite all his hard work in theatre and movies, Eric declared that: 'Most things happen to me by chance. My first attempt at a character part was a bit of luck. Terence Rattigan had written *The Browning Version* and was having difficulty finding a leading actor for the part of Crocker-Harris, the middle-aged schoolmaster at a public boys' school. Five turned down the part.'

The drama was actually called *Playbill* which comprised two plays – *The Browning Version* and *Harlequinade* – performed consecutively on the same night by the same cast. Although Rattigan originally wrote them for the actor John Gielgud, the latter declined, commenting, rather tactlessly, that he "…couldn't take chances with second-rate plays." As can be expected, this upset the playwright, causing a rift between the two which would last many years. So Rattigan approached several other actors including Eric, who had appeared in a film he had co-written called *Escape To Danger*.

Eric later recalled: 'In desperation, I suppose, he offered it to me. How could I hope to portray a middle-aged man? I decided to turn (it) down. I went to Rattigan's chambers, and there, thanks to a large whisky and soda and Mr Rattigan's charm, I found myself agreeing to play the part.'

Also, as Michael Darlow points out in his brilliant book *Terence Rattigan: The Man and his Work*, Eric had previously turned down the lead role in Rattigan's play *The Winslow Boy* (as had John Gielgud), which had then gone on to great success with Emlyn Williams in the lead role, and Eric obviously didn't want to make the same mistake again. So he accepted the lead roles of Andrew Crocker-Harris in *The Browning Version* and Arthur Gosport in *Harlequinade*, while Mary Ellis played his wife in both plays.

The Browning Version is set in a public school, and is based on the emotional repression of an introverted character, schoolmaster Andrew Crocker-Harris, who has heart trouble and is being coerced into early retirement. In his eighteen years at the school, he has gone from being an admired and brilliant scholar to one held in contempt by both his fellow teachers and his pupils, who nickname him 'The Himmler of the Lower Fifth'. This has affected his marriage and his wife is turning her attentions elsewhere. As she tells her lover: 'You can't hurt Andrew. He's dead.' He is due to award a prize to the cricket team and give a speech, but is talked out of doing so and backs down.

However, despite all the negativity towards him, one of his students gives him a present, a copy of his favourite play, and this one act of kindness, encourages him to award the prize and give the speech after all, thereby regaining a little self-respect.

Harlequinade (originally titled *Perdita*) concerns the husband-and-wife theatrical team of Arthur Gosport and Edna Selby, in rehearsal for their performance of *Romeo and Juliet*, with Arthur and Edna playing the title roles, and Arthur directing. Mr Darlow describes the basis of the play as the couple "…needle each other in rehearsal, and wheedle to get their own way, while keeping up a front of mutual admiration and adoration."

At a later date, Rattigan described *Harlequinade* as nothing more than '…a soufflé designed to round off a meal, of which the main course was *The Browning Version*,' adding that if he ever had to justify his career as a playwright, then *The Browning Version* would be the play he would choose as his masterpiece.

After a short pre-London tour, *Playbill* opened on 8th September 1948 at the Phoenix Theatre. It was an immediate success with audiences and critics alike. For the second year running, Rattigan received the Ellen Terry Award for the best new play, and Eric Portman won the award for best actor, presented to him by the Duke of Edinburgh. The critics thought both plays were perfectly judged and *Playbill* ran for eighteen months.

The Daily Mail's reviewer said that in both plays Rattigan's '..acute perceptive talent pierced to the very essence of his characters. One is looking at the workings of real human souls.'

The theatre critic Harold Hobson wrote: 'As one listens wearily night after night to the banal, clipped, naturalistic dialogue of the modern drama, one's heart cries out for writing of courage and colour, for the evocative word and the mannered phrase. But Mr Rattigan makes one doubt the necessity of that cry. In *The Browning Version* there is not a single sentence that in itself would raise the emotional level of a railway timetable. There is hardly a word out of place in giving an order for a pound of vegetables. Yet the audience is moved to tears. And when Crocker-Harris makes his act of defiance at the end of the play, the heart responds as to the sound of a trumpet. It is not, Mr Rattigan reminds us, the intrinsic quality of the words that matter, but the amount and nature of the emotion they can be made to convey. Mr Portman's playing is as quiet as Mr Rattigan's writing. There is a moment in the play when Mr Portman hesitates, polishing his glasses. The action is barely perceptible, but Mr Portman makes it show how all the pride of a man's life can be killed at one blow.'

T. C. Worsley wrote: 'Mr Eric Portman gives one of the brilliant performances of the year. He keeps and holds very exactly the details of the personality, the tics of speech and the uncontrollable jerks of mannerism which a lifetime has stamped on the mask; then when he reaches the moment for the real man to break through, he triumphantly avoids the mawkish.'

A newspaper report, dated 9th October 1948, read: 'One place in London where, it appears, one can hear the broad accents of Yorkshire, almost any evening, is in the vicinity of the Phoenix Theatre, where Eric Portman is playing in Terence Rattigan's *Playbill*. It is Mr Portman's first West End stage appearance, after several years in films, and many Halifax people, visiting London, take the opportunity of calling on the Halifax-born star. They have had a welcome, for Mr Portman retains a keen interest in his home town. He is naturally pleased with the success his stage reappearance is enjoying. "After all these years in films, I was not sure I would like the theatre again," he told a colleague. "But audiences have been so appreciative, one can't help enjoy it".'

Another person to see *The Browning Version* at this time was Irene Holloway, who contacted me after my appeal in *The Stage*. She says: 'From the moment I saw him in *The 49th Parallel*, I became a devoted admirer. After many years working on his film career, he decided to return to the theatre. I attended the first night of *The Browning Version* and found his performance was a revelation. His (portrayal) of the unhappy teacher was so tender, more so when one of his pupils gave him a book, which reduced him to tears. I had never seen an actor cry on stage before, and I thought then that he had been away (from the theatre) for too long. From then on, I was at every first night.'

My media appeal for information about Eric and, in particular, his Fan Club, resulted in a letter from Betty Hooper, who told me: 'In the 1940s I was a teenager and an avid fan of Eric Portman. I joined his fan club, much to the amusement of my friends who were much more into the American idols of the time, but it didn't deter me. I found Eric Portman fascinating and I would travel miles to see his films when they were released – often more than just once. The highlight of my teenage years was when I saw him in person on stage in Portsmouth, appearing in *Separate Tables*, (a later double-drama from Rattigan) with Dorothy Tutin – to me, a quite magical evening. I would very much like to learn more about the man who gave me so much pleasure both on film and on the stage.'

Another lady, Jill Basten, told me: 'As a teenager in the 1940s, I was potty about Eric Portman. But I didn't know he had a fan club – Drat! I had the good fortune to see him in *The Browning Version* and *Harlequinade*. His (portrayal of) Crocker-Harris was even more heartbreaking than Redgrave's performance in the film version. As I lived in London, near where he lived in Chelsea, I even haunted his doorstep hopefully – no luck! – though I was surrounded by posh cinemas and 'fleapits', and was able to catch all his films. Films I could recite forwards, backwards and sideways including *Squadron Leader X*, *The 49th Parallel*, *Wanted For Murder* (a most underrated and excellent film), *Corridor of Mirrors* (again most excellent), *Dear Murderer*, *The Mark of Cain* and those regularly shown on TV now. I was also fortunate enough to see him on stage in *The Blind Goddess* and again in the film.' Years later, Jill visited his grave at St Veep, took a photo and "…said a few thankyous for all the pleasure his performances gave me."

I was contacted by several people who told me of their once-only meeting with Eric, and one such person was Beryl Marston.

'In 1948/1949, when I was 18/19 years old, I was working for Popham's Department Store in Plymouth. During the war, the building had been hit and damaged, and so each department was allocated a small outlet in different parts of the city. Popham's continued to trade in this way for many years. The men's department, where I was employed as a sales assistant, was located in an area called Mutley Plain.'

'One day, a gentleman came into my department and I was shocked and surprised to see it was Eric Portman. He asked me about the Plymouth Blitz and, as I described it, he seemed very interested in what I told him. In the end, he bought a few items of clothing, including a beautiful pink shirt and matching tie, and then said Goodbye and left.'

'He was a true gentleman; very good mannered and courteous. I was overjoyed and could not wait to tell all my friends. They were very jealous of me and it was a time I will never forget. Being a young girl and meeting someone so famous, it has continued to live in my memory and it always shall.'

Also a young girl, Lynn Hudson was an evacuee during the war and was sent to a house in Beverston, Devon. She remembers Eric Portman coming to the village several times during the war years, and visiting the house of local man Stuart Beesley. Unfortunately, I can find no further information on this subject. Irene cannot add much else, other than a distinct memory of how Eric was wearing a sleeveless yellow pullover. She tells me: "It was very unusual for any man to wear such bright coloured clothes as most men tended to wear darker shades."

No doubt Eric was seen and recognised by many of his fans whilst he was resident in London, and Pat Hursey was one of them. She told me: 'I passed him in Shaftesbury Avenue in 1948. I was too shy to say 'hello'. He looked exactly like he did on screen.'

Eric later commented that he didn't think he looked much like he did on screen, but people still recognised him. He related a story to a journalist about how he was driving to his home at Penpol from London, and pulled up at the roadside for a break, when '...out of nowhere, a man poked his head in the car and said: " 'Scuse me, would you be Trevor 'Oward?" I didn't feel like introducing myself, so I said: 'No, I'm sorry. I'm not.' Upon which he retired to the other side of the road and continued to stare at me with a puzzled expression on his face.'

Eric's trips back to Halifax seemed to be fairly frequent, and I think it is reasonably safe to assume they were never less than once a year. There is a cutting, which I assume is from the *Halifax Courier and Guardian*, dated Saturday October 29th 1949, which shows Eric pictured as guest of honour opening the Autumn Fayre at All Souls Church Hall, in

Eric meets friends (top) and his brother Leslie and sister-in-law Alice (below) on a visit to Halifax
(Both photographs courtesy of the Halifax Courier Ltd)

119

Halifax, where he helped to form concert party The Aristocrats while still a teenager. He is pictured with the Reverend A. Simmons, two other men and his sister Winifred, (named as Mrs Winnie Aked), who was now married to Mr Thomas Aked and living in nearby Bradford.

While there are quite a few references in this book about Eric's younger brother Leslie, who ran the family business, (and whose sons John and Michael offered me much help in my research), I could find no further reference to Winifred, and nothing whatsoever about Eric's older brother Clifford, other than the fact that he worked as an Inspector with Castleford Labour Exchange (the old name for the Jobcentre). I didn't think I would discover anything more about him, until Pamela Moll answered my media appeal and wrote: 'My Dad was manager of the Labour Exchange in Barnsley, and Clifford was a visiting Inspector. So my Mum said: "Bring him back for tea." This was during the war and before we moved to Wakefield in 1943. As a curious teenager, I was told not to pry about Eric, as it was rude! However, when I saw Clifford's profile, I blurted out to him: 'Yes, your brother is like you!' And he smiled. This information is quite irrelevant to your request about Eric, but I could not resist writing to you and saying: 'I knew his brother'!'

Eric's next film was *The Spider and the Fly*, about an unusual love triangle which develops between two criminals and a police officer, in 1913, on the eve of World War One. Eric plays Parisian Chief of Police, Fernand Maubert, who is involved with Madeleine Saincaize (Nadia Gray), the accomplice to a suave and successful safecracker Philippe Lodocq (Guy Rolfe). The cast includes George Cole (from TV's *Minder*) as Maubert's assistant, Maurice Denham as Colonel de la Roche, and an early role as a town clerk for Arthur Lowe (Captain Mainwaring in TV's *Dad's Army*).

The journalist Edith Nepean met Eric while he was filming in Paris and wrote: 'Suave, fascinating, polished Eric Portman loves Paris and Continental life, and yet he is essentially British and enormously proud of the fact that he is a Yorkshireman. That 'man of the world' air about him compels interest. He is witty, amusing and a fine conversationalist, so that he is always a welcome guest, and his friendship is greatly valued. In these somewhat gloomy days, it is always refreshing to meet someone who really has the power to coax a smile or a wholehearted laugh.'

In December 1949, the journalist Leonard Wallace noted that unlike many of his contemporaries, Eric liked to constantly switch between films and stage plays, pointing out that every time the actor gave a 'significant' performance in a movie, he either took a rest period or returned to his first love – the theatre. Wallace referred to him as '…one of the problem figures of British pictures, regularly doing work of distinction in them, but never quite belonging to them.' He also stated that despite the majority of Eric's screen characters being 'murderers and other dirty dogs', he retained a feminine following stronger than virtually any other British actor.

He wrote: 'This part is possibly the most interesting one Portman has landed. It presents him with the sympathy that so often in the past he has had to win out of some strange inner quality that has shone through even his most black-hearted villains. Undoubtedly, women once again will enthuse over his performance. Let's see if we can discover a reason why.'

'I think the quality that women admire in Portman is his suggestion of strength of character. Something of his own Yorkshire toughness of spirit seeps through into all his characterisations, even into his psychopathic murderers.'

'But strength is not enough to claim feminine affection. It is strength being harried and tested by circumstances that really gets the girls suffering for him. In *Daybreak*, for instance, as the hangman husband, devoted to a weak and faithless wife, you saw him as a strong character being battered by bitter circumstances. In the most extreme instance, *Wanted For Murder*, the strength was there again, but warped, sapped and finally overthrown by insanity. In *The Spider and the Fly*, the strength is menaced by unrequited love. Quietly, stubbornly, with dignity, Portman suffers – (as do) the ladies in the audience. No one is better than Portman at expressing with a haunted, tortured expression of the eyes in a face, otherwise taut and immobile, the inner bitterness in a strong man's soul.'

'He didn't get that gift of winning sympathy by accident. Years of hard work in the theatre, a long apprenticeship which included plenty of Shakespeare and touring, have given him an assured technique that is second nature. There is ease and authority in his acting these days, and that rare instinct for planting an outburst of emotion in a quiet and controlled performance so that it blazes like an ignited flare with dramatic suddenness.' (Courtesy of Halifax Courier Ltd)

'Portman is most certainly an artist; and that being so, he will probably remain the problem boy of British pictures. For as an artist he will please himself, and will not be tied by normal film contracts. That will be very good for his work – although a little hard on the ladies who want their Portman un-rationed.'

Eric's old friend, Eric Moorcroft, recalled an evening in October 1949, during a social gathering at All Souls' Church School, at Haley Hill, Halifax, in which Eric paid a flying visit.

'There, Mr Portman delighted the many parishioners who remembered his own early stage efforts, notably when he helped to form a concert party, 'The Aristocrats' at All Souls, and afterwards produced a play called *The Magic Key*.'

'I remember as soon as he stepped

Leslie, Alice and Eric in a publicity pose for the *Yorkshire Post* newspaper (By kind courtesy of Yorkshire Post Newspapers Ltd)

from the platform, he chatted with 90-year-old Kate Halliday of Salisbury Place, Ackroydon, then the oldest member of the church. He also renewed acquaintance with Mr Edgar Smith, former Mayor of Halifax (and founder of the Halifax Motor Company), and another veteran member of All Souls'.

Edgar Smith recalled: 'Mr Portman told me that evening that he was flying to Egypt on the following Friday to make a new film, *The Poison Road*, a drama based on the traffic in narcotic drugs. In that film, he was to play the role of Yousseff Bey, the Chief of the Egyptian Police.'

The film was released in 1950 under the new title *Cairo Road* and concerns a team of Egyptian anti-narcotic agents attempting to prevent the shipment of drugs crossing the southern border of Egypt, which gives the film its title.

The film was directed by David MacDonald, and it co-starred Lawrence Harvey, Karel Stepanek, Harold Lang, Peter Jones and also featured John Gregson in an early role as a coastguard, who later found fame in films like *Genevieve*, with Kenneth More.

After work on the film ended, Eric returned to the stage, and on Tuesday 23rd May 1950, at the Prince's Theatre, Eric played the title role in *His Excellency*, written by Dorothy and Campbell Christie and directed by Charles Hickman.

'Another fluke,' Eric later told a journalist. 'Just as in *The Browning Version*, again several leading actors turned down the part. Then it was offered to me and someone suggested that I should ask the authors to change the role of the Governor, which was written for a Cockney, into a Yorkshireman. This they agreed to do and I accepted the part.'

Theatre critic T. C. Worsley wrote: 'The evening is a triumph for Mr Portman. (He) provides something here that is unusual on the English stage – a star performance that is nevertheless not a personality performance. This is the art of acting from the inside of a character at its highest and Mr Portman keeps it up all the way through the play. Not one gesture or inflection is commonplace or conventional. Every detailed touch contributes; every movement is genuinely in that part.'

In 2011, Betty Breheny sent me a copy of the theatre programme, which she had saved from a certain evening – sixty-one years ago – when she and her husband had seen the play during their honeymoon in 1950. She told me: 'You are welcome to keep this programme, otherwise, when I am gone, my family will look at it and say: "Eric Portman? Who's Eric Portman?"'

The then prime minister Clement Atlee had seen Eric's performance in the play. After the show, he went backstage to meet him and told the actor – somewhat cryptically: 'You know, in your make-up – you look like Arthur Deakin – and you talk like George Tomlinson.' (*Deakin was a trade unionist and Tomlinson a politician with the Labour Party).

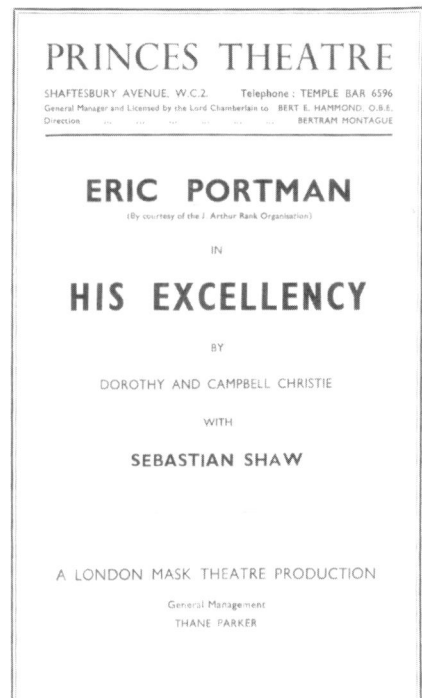

Having seen Eric's performance in *Playbill*, Irene Holloway attended the first night of *His Excellency* at the

left: Eric heads the cast of the stage play *His Excellency*
(Courtesy of the Prince of Wales Theatre)
below: Advertising the play *His Excellency*
(Courtesy of the Adephi Theatre)

Shaftesbury. She told me: 'This was the first time I got to know him and I was able to see him again and again. At the time, there were photographs of the cast displayed outside the theatre and I discovered that the photographer lived a short distance away in Covent Garden, so I went along to his studio and bought a very nice 10" x 8" photo of Eric. I visited the theatre after the performance and asked Eric to sign it for me which he duly did. He asked me how much I had paid for it and I told him 7 shillings and sixpence. He put his hand on my shoulder and said 'That was very kind of you.' From then on, I would be invited to his dressing room and treated as a friend.'

By 1950, Eric was widely considered to be the pre-eminent Yorkshire actor and one of the highest paid film heart-throbs in the country. On 3rd January 1951, Eric appeared as a guest on the BBC Radio series *Desert Island Discs*, presented by Roy Plomley. On the BBC website it says that the programme is not currently available to hear, but this implies that it may be available one day, so it may be worth returning to the website to check, from time to time. His musical choices (full list in the bibliography section), included Jean Sablon's Parisian song *Le Fiacre*, the Merry Widow Waltz and *A Voice in the Night* which was from Eric's film *Wanted For Murder*.

His Excellency ran from May 1950 to November 1951 – another example of why the actor earned his nickname 'Long-Run Eric,' and rather than taking a break, he got cast in another stage production, playing Sir Robert Bistrow, MP, in Royston Morley's play *The Guilty Party*, which toured the country, including the Theatre Royal, Nottingham. Edward Motteram told me he would never forget a very enjoyable evening watching the performance and he recalls other actors in the cast such as Frances Ryland and Terence Alexander (the latter of whom would later portray Charlie Hungerford in TV's *Bergerac*).

Later that year, Eric returned to Halifax, helping with fundraising for his old school, Holy Trinity, and shortly after, he played The Marshall in Peter

Ustinov's play *The Moment of Truth*, which had quite a short run. One reviewer wrote of Eric's character: 'This old man is nothing but an old bore and though Eric Portman does everything he can technically to make us feel about him, we can pass through the last part of the play almost wholly untouched.' Incidentally, the cast included Brian Wilde (who would later find fame on TV, playing Mr Barraclough in *Porridge* and Foggy Dewhirst in *The Last of the Summer Wine*).

Despite the relatively short run of the play, it appears that the company toured Britain, including a performance at the Grand Theatre, Leeds. On 23rd October 1952, less than an hour after the curtain came down, it was reported that Eric visited The Grand Theatre, Halifax, to meet for the first time members of the Halifax Playgoers Club, of which he had agreed to become the president. Mr Portman called for a greater recognition of the professional actor as opposed to the amateur player. The professional theatre, he said, must be an important centre in a town, and drama must be done by professionals. Eric told the members: 'There is a great chasm between the amateur and the professional player. No actor is an actor if he just does it as something extra and is doing a different job. The amateur stage is a help to the community, but it does not take the part of the professional stage.'

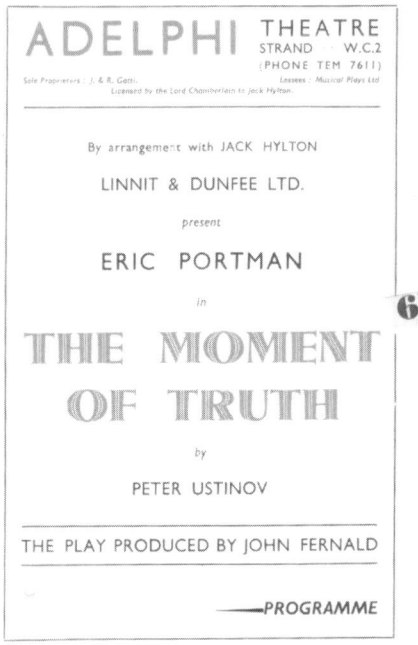

Eric stars in Peter Usinov's stage play *The Moment of Truth* (Courtesy of the Adephi Theatre)

He also criticised theatre producers who staged revivals of the old classics. 'These are an easy way out,' he said. 'What people want today is contemporary drama. We should find new plays about modern life. Why not a (local) competition… for people to write new plays? Surely there might be a Bronte or a Priestley in Halifax?'

That year, Eric's next film appearance was in *The Magic Box*, a biographical drama – or 'biopic' – made in 1951, and directed by John Boulting for the British Lion Film Corporation. This was a project for the *Festival of Britain*, and adapted from the controversial biography of William Friese-Greene. He was the first person to design and patent a working cinematic camera, hence the title *The Magic Box*. It starred Robert Donat as Friese-Greene and the story, told in flashback, recounts the inventor's countless experiments with the 'moving image', charting his many failures and disappointments, and showing how others attempted to take the credit for his discoveries. Eric plays the part of Arthur Collings, the Yorkshire businessman, who first commercialised Friese-Greene's talents. He told a newspaper that he was delighted at the opportunity to appear in the film, not only because he was anxious to 'do his bit' towards this film industry project, but also because the part '…gave him the chance of portraying an honest-to-goodness character from his own county, after a succession of somewhat grim roles!'

This is one of the few films since *The 49th Parallel*, where Eric is not one of the top-billed performers. Indeed, it was one of those occasional star-studded movies, where not only the leads are famous but also the supporting cast and even many of the bit-part players were household names. The cast list reads like a 'Who's Who of the Cinema' and the main supporting cast included Maria Schell, John Howard Davies, Robert Beatty, Richard Attenborough, Bernard Miles, Joyce Grenfell, Dennis Price, Margaret Rutherford, Mervyn Johns and Glynis Johns, while the multitude of cameos included: Cecil Parker, David

Tomlinson, Ronald Shiner, Emlyn Williams, Ernest Thesiger, Kay Walsh, Leo Genn, Laurence Olivier, Jack Hulbert, Marius Goring, Michael Denison, Michael Hordern, Miles Malleson, Peter Ustinov, Sheila Sim, Sid James, Stanley Holloway, Thora Hird, Googie Withers, Richard Murdoch, Sybil Thorndike and William Hartnell (who later played the first Doctor in TV's *Doctor Who*).

Although it was completed and shown just before the end of the Festival, it wasn't given general release to the public until 1952 and was nominated for two BAFTAs that year, for Best Film and Best British Film.

Around this time, a journalist wrote that Eric '…has light brown hair, hazel eyes and is five-feet-eleven inches tall. In private life, he prefers to avoid crowds and parties and likes to relax in the quiet of his own home. He has a flat in London and a cottage in a Cornish fishing village to which he goes at every possible moment. His favourite pastimes are swimming, talking and reading. His favourite authors are Somerset Maugham and Evelyn Waugh, and you will always find a well-worn series of Shakespeare's plays within easy reach of his armchair. Eric has travelled a great deal and has visited nearly every European country. He admits to a superstition about the number thirteen. He is intensely interested in the acting profession, and he is always ready to give a young artiste any help he can. In the film studios, he is regarded as one of the most unassuming of actors. He is quite willing to dispense with a stand-in, and between scenes he will attend to his own make-up. He is the delight of any director, for he grasps very quickly the essentials of the part he is to play.'

Less than a year after Eric appeared in the stage play of *His Excellency*, he was cast in the same role in the film version. As in *One of Our Aircraft is Missing*, *Millions Like Us*, *The Magic Box*, and a later film *The Good Companions*, he is cast as a Yorkshireman, sent to take over the post of Governor on a British-ruled island in the Mediterranean.

Also in the cast are Cecil Parker, Helen Cherry, Edward Chapman, Clive

Morton, Geoffrey Keen and Robin Bailey. Directed by Robert Hamer for Ealing Studios, this is classed as an 'Ealing Comedy', alongside more well known films in the series such as *The Lavender Hill Mob* and *Passport to Pimlico*.

After the film was released, a journalist wrote that: '(Eric) has no time for the present studio fashion among stars, of pretending that you prefer the stage to the screen. His more recent 'bad-man' roles have not affected his quiet, likeable personality. Any man who is fond of a garden and country life as he is, is bound to be mellow and popular and fit easily into any company, just as he fits easily into the oldest sweater and baggiest trousers he can find for his relaxation away from it all. Comfortable, you'd call his clothes on these occasions – and easy and comfortable their wearer. But not smug. Success has not spoiled the Yorkshire lad from behind a counter. He is never far away in memory from those dreary nights in theatrical digs, and he has never ceased being grateful to find himself famous.'

'For the last three years, (Eric) has refused to work in a film studio and a theatre at the same time. By sticking to this principle, he lost out to Michael Redgrave for the schoolmaster part in *The Browning Version*. And nobody more than Portman wanted to play the role he created in Rattigan's *Playbill*, and for which he won the Ellen Terry Prize as the best British stage actor in 1948.'

'But Portman was adamant. "I cannot do justice to both jobs," he said. Portman's danger to my mind, though, comes when he does undertake both jobs. For instance, his latest film, *His Excellency*, was received rather coolly for a Portman vehicle. Maybe it wasn't his fault, but after his handling of the part on stage, the screen edition came up like dusty chromium plating. Perhaps that's one fragment of the Portman puzzle that will never be satisfactorily explained.'

Eric rarely played the same types of characters in concurrent plays and films, and so in his next movie he went for a complete change, as an archaeologist in an adventure movie, which was set – and filmed on location – in Algiers.

While it was released to British cinemas in March 1953 under the rather limp title *South of Algiers*, it was subsequently released in the US, exactly a year later, as *The Golden Mask*.

Eric plays Dr Burnet, a scholar of ancient history at the British Museum, who is obsessed with finding a legendary and priceless treasure called The Golden Mask of Moloch, believed to be buried in the Algerian desert. However, as he is low on funds, he cannot afford to pay an archaeologist to accompany him, and has to make do with Nicholas Chapman (played by Van Heflin), an author of archaeology books, who offers to come along without payment. Burnet agrees to this, but is highly suspicious of Chapman's motives.

The movie has a bit of everything from villains in the guise of unscrupulous fortune hunter Petris (Charles Golder) and his assistant Kress (Jacques B. Brunius), to a blossoming romance between Chapman and Burnet's daughter, Anne, (Wanda Hendrix) who accompanies them on the expedition, together with some infighting between Chapman and Anne's current beau Jacques (Jacques Francois), in addition to a rocky friendship between Burnet and Chapman, with the latter finally proving his worth as the hero saving the day.

When the film was released, a journalist asked Eric: 'How did you like filming in Africa?'

'I was glad of the opportunity to travel,' he replied. 'But we experienced very rough weather, which prevented us from looking around as much as we would have liked. However, that had its advantages: it brought Van Heflin and I together and we got to know each other really well. Some people found Mr Heflin an aggressive man and they thought he and I would clash, but we got on splendidly and formed a friendship which I think will last.'

A press cutting at the time stated that '…while filming on location in Africa … (Eric) was constantly in demand as "technical adviser" on camel-riding – because of his previous experience with camels when in Egypt for the film *Cairo Road*.'

Quite how he found the time to make these two movies when he was still under contract to play the MP Robert Bristow in *The Guilty Party*, I do not know, though he would understandably tell friends and family that he longed for a break. When the play went on tour, with one of the venues being the Lyceum Theatre, in Sheffield, Eric had a reunion with his family backstage after the performance.

A local newspaper reported that: 'The reunion began with a few relatives, including uncle John Edward Portman, of Langsett, (aged 83 in December) who always sees Eric when he appears locally. But when the invasion started, the dressing-room seemed scarcely large enough to hold all the cousins and others who called to wish him good luck.'

'You must find this rather overpowering,' said one, as Eric shook hands with them. 'Not at all,' he replied. 'It's exactly what I hoped would happen.'

But among it all, Eric was relieved. The strain of playing again in Sheffield, among his 'own' people, was 'tremendous', he said. The conclusion,

A family reunion at the Lyceum Theatre, Sheffield, where Eric is appearing in *The Guilty Party* (source unknown)

however, was that the audience had been the most sophisticated the company had yet played to on their tour. He said: 'They took the play just the right way; the tenseness was reflected in their silence, and it wasn't until the curtain was down, that we knew what that silence really meant.'

After another performance, he took the opportunity to pop over to see his cousins in the village of Thorpe Hesley, near Rotherham, where his father had been born. On Thursday 16th October 1952, he met up with his aunt Sarah Jane Portman (nee Smith) at her home – The Cottage, Wentworth Road, in the village. She had been unable to travel to the Lyceum to see the show, so Eric had paid a visit. He also met other cousins Clarence, Anne and Harold Portman (the latter a well-known local amateur actor) and another cousin, Mrs Phyllis Chesman, who later told a reporter that Eric 'was quite a gentleman and had a very lovable nature.'

Eric visits his Aunty and cousins at Thorpe Hesley, near Rotherham

Over lunch at Mrs Portman's home, Eric recalled many holiday visits there as a young boy and recalled old characters of the village who had now died. Later in the day, he went to visit another cousin, Mr Friend Portman, of Hesley Bar, who worked as the Men's Checkweighman at the Smithywood Colliery of Messrs. Newton Chambers and Co. Ltd.

Although Eric's cousin, Harold, had been at the family reunion in Thorpe Hesley, there was another later meeting which he was unable to attend, and Eric wrote the following letter to him:

Next Week:-
Grand Theatre,
Wolverhampton

My dear Harold,

   I was delighted to get your letter this morning – especially as we missed seeing you on Wednesday – that was a big disappointment!

   I did so want to get over again to Thorpe to see you all but somehow things have gone wrong – and I haven't been able to have even a meal alone. It's a dreadful thing to be for ever busy Harold!

   I'm looking forward now – every day – to my vacation which comes about the beginning of June. It will be wonderful to be amongst you all – and I shall be able to have a quiet holiday in the fields – You will have to show me all the best walks and we shall be able to talk over things together.

   Isn't Clarence a big lad now – I'm afraid I felt very small in comparison!

   And Phyllis, of course, is quite a lady!

   Tell Auntie and Uncle I am writing to them – and say I can still remember the taste of those little yellow tarts!

        With all my love

        Your affectionate cousin

        Eric

The play toured to other theatres in Yorkshire, including his home town of Halifax, and I received a letter from another of the actor's cousins, who had seen him perform there. And this cousin was *another* Eric Portman!

He writes: 'My name is Eric Portman and I was born on 12th February 1941 in Stocksbridge, South Yorkshire. My father Albert Portman was the only son of my Grandfather John Edward Portman and the family home was in

Langsett, near Sheffield. He had a brother called Matthew who was a tailor in Halifax and was the father of my famous namesake. They also had two sisters, Ada and Eva, who both lived to a ripe old age in Langsett, and Ada kept up a correspondence with Eric, giving him the family news.'

'As family stories go, there was a problem in finding a name for me when I was born. I think it was my grandfather who decided that I should be called Eric, after our relative who was, by then, a very successful stage and screen actor. Having this famous name had no effect on me, although it was instantly recognised by many people in the period from 1940 through to the 1960s.'

'Some time in 1952, at the age of 11 years, I was taken to the theatre in Halifax, to see my namesake in a play. I had just passed my eleven-plus so I proudly wore my new school uniform for this auspicious occasion. I clearly remember climbing on the charabanc and setting off for Halifax for the evening performance. We were in the cheaper seats, high up in the 'Gods', but I have no recollection of the play save for the huge applause given to my namesake when he walked onto the stage. It puzzled me why this should be so. He hadn't even said a word at this point!'

'After the performance, Aunt Ada said that we had been invited to visit the actor in his dressing room and we were ushered down and down until we came to a room full of people, all talking and drinking. I remember the lights and the ubiquitous make-up mirror. After a short period of family pleasantries, someone said: 'Eric – we would like you to meet your namesake.' I went to the front and the two Eric Portmans sat, side by side, in front of the lighted mirror. All I can remember vividly was Eric saying that we ought to work out our relationship. He took a pen and paper out of the desk and drew a family tree, concluding that: "You and I are cousins to the second place removed."'

'I had no idea what that meant!'

'Then he opened another drawer and my eyes must have popped out because I had never seen so much money before – crisp, white £5 notes, £1 notes and 10/- notes.'

'Eric took out one of the £1 notes, put it in the pocket of my new school blazer, and patted it, saying: 'Here's something to remember me by.'

'And at that – I burst into tears!'

'There were no other meetings or memories after that. I moved to Devon in 1974 and discovered that Eric had lived – and died – in Cornwall, near Lostwithiel. My wife Jane and I did eventually find his memorial stone in St Veep churchyard, and we visit occasionally, taking a flower from our garden here in Tavistock as something for *him* to remember *me* by!'

Eric Portman – *our* Eric – returned to Wyndham's Theatre, London, to play Father James Brown, in Graham Greene's controversial play *The Living Room*. The previous year he had reportedly agreed to appear in a film, *Pleasure Island*, for Paramount in Hollywood, playing 'the father of two girls', but for whatever reason, it was either never made, or maybe released under a different title with a different cast and I can find no other record of it.

In August 1953, the journalist R. Quilter Vincent met up with Eric at Wyndham's Theatre, during rehearsals for *The Living Room*. The actor suggested they go for a drink, so the two made their way to the Scotch Ale gin house, accompanied by Eric's secretary Harry McLarnon, who Vincent describes as 'a pleasant middle-aged Irishman.'

Eric chose a small table in the corner of the bar and said (wrongly, as it turned out): 'We will not be disturbed here.'

Vincent describes Eric as: 'Tall, plumpish, and heavy featured. He has dark blue eyes and receding snow-white hair brushed straight back. One might have recognised him by his unusual voice, which is resonant and slightly nasal, but with not a trace of the Yorkshire accent he can assume to perfection when he likes. He has a charming personality, but I suspect that he is a very practical man with not much time for sentiment. It would be very difficult, I should say, to put one over on Mr Portman.'

Vincent pointed out that *The Living Room* was outspoken about some subjects including religion and sex, and Eric replied: '*The Living Room* is the most outspoken play I've come across. It concerns a Roman Catholic girl who falls in love with, and becomes the mistress of, a married man of the Protestant faith. A Roman Catholic priest and a psychiatrist try but fail to help solve her problem and she commits suicide. The play is by Graham Greene – the first one he has written directly for the stage. As you know, Mr Greene is currently very much in vogue as the author of numerous successful films, including *The Third Man*.'

Eric was playing the part of a priest confined to a wheelchair and he said that some had advised him against taking a part so similar to the one he had played, less than a year ago, in Peter Ustinov's *The Moment of Truth*, in which he portrayed an elderly man, almost entirely confined to a wheelchair.

When the journalist recalled a previous conversation with Ustinov, on the point that the play may not have been a success because it was put on at an unsuitable theatre, Eric Portman said: 'I'm sure you're right. It's a pity Peter didn't choose a smaller house. However, I regret nothing, certainly not my appearance in *The Moment of Truth*. The play's had a long run in several other places like Germany.'

Vincent asked if Eric found that plays which enjoyed such long runs become tedious and Eric agreed. But he added that even as the enthusiasm for the part diminishes over a play's long-run, that that the quality of performance must not diminish at any cost.

'It is a matter of integrity that the actor continues to give of his best,' said Eric. 'After all, audiences pay for their seats.'

As the pair talked, a bald-headed gentleman in dishevelled clothing, who had come to sit at the table a few minutes before, leaned forward and said: 'Good evening, sir,' to Eric, adding, somewhat incongruously: 'I know you, don't I?'

'Eric returned the 'Good Evening' with a smile. The man hesitated for an instant, then said: 'Could I get you to buy an old man a drink?'

The journalist points out that this 'old' man cannot have been older than forty-five.

'Certainly,' said Eric. 'What are you drinking?'

'That's very nice of you,' said the newcomer. 'A mild if you please.'

Eric's secretary stood up and went over to the bar to order another round of drinks, including a mild beer for the guest.

The journalist mentioned the film *South of Algiers*, which was shortly due to be released in the cinemas, remarking that Eric was not making as many films as he did years ago, and the actor agreed, saying that parts he were offered in the theatre often proved too attractive to resist, and that it would be nice to get offered what he termed as 'more strong, vigorous type parts,' such as those he had played in *The 49th Parallel* and *Squadron Leader X*. He added that he had learned much from his part in the former of the two: 'I learned that often it is possible to achieve greater realism and effect by playing a character in a fashion contrary to what is generally expected. You remember I was a Nazi U-boat Commander in the film? Well instead of making him a raging braggart, I sought to emphasise the virtues of the man, and played him sympathetically. It had the effect of making some people think I was a Nazi! So with the Roman Catholic priest in my next play, *The Living Room*, I shall not portray him as a man of superhuman understanding and ability, but as an ordinary being, with human failings, hopes and fears. Now, I shall live the part of the priest for the next few weeks.'

'I look at things this way – I'm a lucky man. I have the job I wanted and I'm favoured with success, so the very least I can do is study and play to the best of my ability any part I take on. But I try to do more than that. I experiment and I accept challenges in my work in order to make myself as interesting as I know how. Acting is my whole life, you see, and I want to give it all I've got.'

I received a letter from Griff Loyd who met Eric whilst the play was showing at Wyndhams. Griff has worked as both an actor and writer in theatre, TV and film productions, but began his career with BBC Radio and his first job was as an interviewer for a Forces Radio programme called *Out and About*. He tells me: 'One particular weekend I was sent around London to pre-arranged venues, accompanied by a recording crew and the show's producer, to interview some of the celebrities of that time. Following an interview with Jimmy Edwards and Tony Hancock at the Adelphi Theatre in the Strand, we were whisked quickly to another West End theatre where I was booked to interview Eric Portman. The date (taken from my old diary) was Saturday 1st August 1953. We met the great man in his dressing room, where the crew went about setting up their equipment and testing the microphone, then sitting me opposite Eric Portman and arming me with a list of questions. Then Eric said: 'Hang on a minute, lads. Before we start, are you thirsty?' There was a murmur of gratitude as he poured some drinks for us. After laughing so much with Jimmy Edwards, my throat was rather dry and needed lubrication. Eric handed me a tumbler half-filled with what I thought was Lucozade – one of my favourites. "Oh, lovely! Thank you," I said, and downed it in one go.'

'Lucozade? WRONG! It was neat whisky! The room erupted in panic as I coughed, spluttered, choked, and sat there, almost unconscious, gasping for air, as they slapped me on the back and tried to revive me. My whole life flashed before me in that one brief moment. My producer said: 'Don't worry, Griff. I'll take over,' and he conducted the interview instead. So I missed out on that one, and all because of my first introduction to neat whisky at the hands of Eric Portman! Hilarious when I think of that incident now – but disastrous at the time.'

In a review of *The Living Room*, the famous theatre critic Kenneth Tynan wrote: 'Though I must applaud Eric Portman's unselfishness in accepting the role of the priest, I must deplore the waste involved. His legs were cut off at the knees and his temperament was cut off at the mains. Mr Portman is an active actor miscast in a passive part.'

CHAPTER 7

CHOOSE A PART FOR PORTMAN

In 1953, *The Picturegoer* magazine ran a competition for its readers called 'Choose A Part for Eric Portman', and the actor was amongst those on the judging panel asked to choose a winner.

The readers were invited to see the film *South of Algiers* and then send suggestions for possible future roles for the actor. The first prize, by arrangement with Associated British Studios, Air France, and the French Line organisation, was a fortnight's stay for two at a luxury hotel in Algiers, flying from Britain by Air France.

The winner was Mrs Barbara Gouldsmith, of Bexhill-On-Sea, who suggested "General Gordon, the Khartoum hero."

Mrs Gouldsmith said she thought of the role while reading a book about Gordon. She and her husband Dick were described as 'keen picturegoers' – and Mr Portman had long been their favourite actor. 'As soon as I thought of Gordon – I knew it was it,' she said.

At Eric's request, the number of consolation prizes was increased from six to nine, to reward others who suggested Gordon – '…except for those whose entries were longer than the rules permitted.' In all other cases where more than one reader put forward a particular role – Lawrence of Arabia, for example – the judges made presentation and clarity of expression the deciding factors. Each of the nine consolation-prize winners were given an all-expenses-paid trip to the Associated British Studios, in Elstree, to watch filming and meet Eric Portman.

Other suggestions for characters included the explorer David Livingstone, the Hanging Judge (Judge Jeffries), and the composer Richard Wagner.

Eric said he was delighted how audiences had keenly sized him up and flattered that they had observed something of which he was secretly proud – versatility. Audiences clearly didn't view him as a 'type', pointing out that he always aimed for variety, '…from the docile priest of my current West End play *The Living Room* to the forceful and embittered man of *South Of Algiers.*'

ERIC PORTMAN

Publicity shot
(© J. Arthur Rank Organisation)

He congratulated the winner, one of several entrants who had suggested General Gordon, whom Eric viewed as a multi-faceted character – strong, but with undercurrents of softness rather than weakness. He pointed out that Gordon was something of a mystic; a combination of idealist and realist – the very depth of personality which makes the role so magnetic to an actor, he said.

Other suggestions included the famous barrister Marshall Hall. 'I'd certainly like to portray Hall,' he said. 'I am sure that in what I may call my 'strong vein,' the part would suit me well. Hall won cases on personality alone, one might say, and that picturesque forcefulness – which all fine lawyers must have in some degree, I suppose – offers big opportunities.'

Eric considered the character of Strickland, in Somerset Maugham's *The Moon and Sixpence*, a 'first-rate idea,' but pointed out it had been done twice before, and that it could probably not be improved upon. Another suggestion was the Reverend Patrick Bronte, father of the Bronte sisters, but he thought the man did not have that many sides to his personality, therefore not making him appealing and intriguing enough for an actor to portray.

Prince Metternich was another suggestion, and Eric said that since he played a Nazi in both *The 49th Parallel* and *Squadron Leader X*, he had always wanted another Teutonic role. 'I like the idea of Metternich,' he said.

'Oh, yes – play myself. That was one reader's suggestion. But I'm a little self-conscious about that!'

Eric told a journalist that he knew that one day he would want to retire. 'I know I would be very content with it. One's outlook changes as time goes by and the way I look at things now is this: I've had a pretty good share of success – I hope I shall continue to have – but if I ever feel that the public is growing tired of me, or that my career as an actor is no longer serving any useful purpose, I shall give it up. I won't make the mistake that quite a lot of actors make of overstaying my time. On the other hand, so long as I feel I'm doing a useful job, I shall carry on. After all, I'm blessed with excellent health – very necessary in this profession – and the parts I get seem to be better than ever; they're incomparably superior to those that were available to me as a young man. Also, I'm fortunate in that I didn't begin to make a name for myself until (quite late) in my life – 40 or thereabouts – consequently, people don't remember me as a young actor and say: 'Oh, isn't he getting old-looking?' I can play men of my own age or a good deal older; I once played a man in his dotage. (*He was probably speaking of

Andrew Crocker-Harris in *The Browning Version*). So you see, it looks like I can go on for years – in fact, the older I get, the wider seems to grow my scope. A rather happy situation, don't you think?'

In February 1954, Eric played Mark Heath in *Shadow of the Vine* at Wyndham's Theatre, London, but it couldn't have resulted in one of Long-Run-Eric's long-term successes, because he spent the rest of the year making two films and a play for TV.

In 1954, Desmond Pratt of the *Yorkshire Post*, wrote an article entitled: 'Eric Portman, a true-to-life actor', and made the following observations:

'Technical accomplishment alone is not enough to produce fine performances in the theatre. There must be about the actor an integrity in his portrayal that can spring only from a close and intelligent observation and appraisement of the life around him. Such a quality is possessed to a full degree by Eric Portman. Sincerity has stamped all the work I have seen him do on the stage. When you meet him, you are immediately impressed by his considerable and unassuming charm, but you are also aware of his deep interest in his profession and in the future of the British theatre. During (the last two decades) he has played many parts, grasped the essentials of his art and brought to bear on his playing that keen and sympathetic observation of life so necessary for the true artist...He stands before us now as a fully matured artist, thoughtful in his interpretations yet powerful both in his moments of repose or action on the stage. Since 1948, Mr Portman has been back on the stage, where the actor, unaided by cameras or cutting rooms, shows his true calibre. It is because he possesses integrity that he has been able to portray characters which, although outside an audience's normal experiences, still have about them the ring of truth. Throughout his busy career, Eric Portman has never forgotten his beginnings. He visits his family two or three times each year. He represents the British theatre at home and abroad at its very best, and he is one of those, by whose example and standards that theatre will be judged. Its heritage, handed down from such figures as Garrick and Irving, is safe in such hands.' (Courtesy of Yorkshire Post Newspapers Ltd)

Eric's next film to be released was *The Colditz Story* (1955), directed and co-written by Guy Hamilton who, like Terence Young, (director of the actor's earlier film *Corridor of Mirrors*,) would also graduate to direct James Bond films. The plot concerns British and other allied soldiers who have escaped from Nazi prison camps, are sent to a supposedly secure prison camp in a castle (or schloss) called Oflag IV-C. Although the soldiers of different nationalities try their own plans, Eric's character, Colonel Redmond, a senior British officer, suggests that they work together to form escape plans. After ridding themselves of a German traitor in their midst, the escapes go ahead. Some successful, some not. John Mills plays British officer Patrick Reid who assists in the escape of other prisoners, before escaping himself. And the cast also includes Lionel Jeffries, Richard Wattis, Ian Carmichael, Anton Diffring (who played many German officers in war films) and Bryan Forbes, who would himself direct Eric in two later films. The movie would later inspire a TV series simply called *Colditz*, starring David McCallum, Robert Wagner, Jack Hedley and Edward Hardwicke.

Eric said later that he only got the part in the movie, because the producer had seen him in a TV play. He wrote: 'I recently did a play called *Jeannie* on the BBC: a nice little comedy-drama in which I played a funny, honest character who showed more tenderness than I had had a chance to reveal in film roles for a long time. Directly, as a result, I was offered the part I have just been doing in *The Colditz Story*, at Shepperton. The role has aspects very much in common with the one in *Jeannie*. TV is a wonderful shop window for actors. Eight million people watch that little screen at home. Among them are casting directors and producers!'

Eric's next film was written by Terence Rattigan, adapting his own stage play. Produced for Twentieth Century Fox, *The Deep Blue Sea* (1955), concerning a wife's infidelity, was directed by Anatole Litvak, and starred Kenneth More and Vivien Leigh, with Eric as the main supporting actor. The cast also featured Emlyn Williams, Moira Lister, Alec McCowen, Dandy Nichols, Jimmy Hanley, Miriam Karlin and Sidney James. It received BAFTA nominations for Litvak, Rattigan and Kenneth More.

Signed photograph (source unknown)

CHAPTER 8

NEVER A NIGHT SO GRAND

Just as Terence Rattigan wrote his first two-handed drama *Playbill* (comprising *Harlequinade* and *The Browning Version*), his new work, *Separate Tables*, also consisted of two plays entitled *Table By The Window* and *Table Number Seven*. As *Playbill* had been written with John Gielgud in mind, which was then snapped up by Eric Portman after the former turned it down, Rattigan then wrote *Separate Tables*, commenting to his New York agent that he had '…a rather exciting idea for two short plays, which might be right for Eric Portman.' Whether or not he wrote them with Eric in mind, is not known for certain, but the actor's success in the previous Rattigan double-bill, and a quote from Eric himself in the next paragraph, rather suggests that he did.

Based on Eric's quotes during interviews that he always aimed to play totally different characters, two-handed dramas such as *Playbill* and *Separate Tables* would have been of extreme interest for him, allowing him to play two contrasting roles within the same evening's performance. 'You don't get anywhere unless you accept challenges,' said Eric. 'This is one reason why I have taken on contrasting roles in two short stage plays that Terence Rattigan has written for me, *Separate Tables*.'

In *Table by the Window*, Eric is cast as John Malcolm, former Labour Leader-turned-journalist, who has been in prison for the attempted murder of his wife. In the play, his wife tracks him down to the hotel where he is staying, and after many arguments, they both conclude that although they have little hope together, they have none apart.

In *Table Number Seven*, Eric plays Major Pollock, an apparently respectable retired soldier. However, It soon transpires that Pollock is hiding a scandal where he was involved with a young woman, and his secret is soon discovered by Mrs Railton-Bell who is staying in the same hotel. Not only is she domineering to the Major, but also to her daughter, Sybil, and both characters feel threatened by her. By the end of the play, all the other guests have rallied around both helpless characters, who then become more confident as a result, and both refusing to be bullied by Mrs Railton-Bell any longer.

Rattigan originally intended the Major's scandal to involve a young man. But at a time when here had been rumours circulating about Eric's private life, the actor told the playwright he did not want to play any openly gay character, which would then fuel any further rumours. He had absolutely no desire to play Pollock as a homosexual. He regarded his sexuality as an entirely private matter between himself and those closest to

Theatre programme of Terence Rattigan's two-handed play *Separate Tables* at the former St James Theatre, London (© St James Theatre)

him. He had no wish to endure the kind of attentions from the police and blackmailers recently suffered by others.

And in such cultural circumstances, Portman's reticence to allow Kenneth Tynan or anyone else to write his biography is also understandable. So he accepted the roles only on the condition that Rattigan rewrote Pollock's scandal as heterosexual in nature. Also, Rattigan's colleague, Bob Whitehead, told the playwright that changing the crime to homosexual, would make his play 'smaller' in a sense, as the whole emphasis of that play would have changed, diminishing the 'universality of its message' of man's inhumanity to man – illustrated in the play, where one character describes Mrs Railton-Bell's savaging of the Major, as similar to that of the McCarthy witch-hunt.

Donald Walker, former manager of the Grand Theatre, Halifax, told me: … "One needs to remember that his time as a leading player on stage and screen came before the more permissive years when actors such as Ian McKellen 'came out' as openly gay men. Remember the horror amongst the tea-cups when John Gielgud was arrested for soliciting; that incident put back his expected knighthood for at least a decade. Many other public figures stepped back into the shadows thinking: 'There but for the grace of God…' so Eric's ultra-discreet private life was very understandable.'

The first performance of *Separate Tables,* directed by Peter Glenville, opened at St James' Theatre, London, on Wednesday 2nd September 1954. Despite Eric's other successful long-running productions, *Separate Tables* would beat all previous – and subsequent – stage productions, running from 1954-1956 in the UK and 1956-1958 in the USA.

Kenneth Tynan reported: 'It is Eric Portman who commands the stage, volcanic as the journalist, but even better as the major, speaking in nervous spasms and walking stiff-legged with his shoulders protectively hunched. He has the mask of the true mime. The comedian as opposed to the actor.'

Writing in *Plays and Players*, Ronald Barker said of *Table By The Window*: 'Eric Portman as the broken-down politician with heavy drooping shoulders, podgy figure, hesitant walk, and rough, unkempt appearance is perfectly in key. The performance is so right that one is apt to take this great talent for granted.'

Of Eric's character in *Table Number Seven*, he added: 'Rattigan sketches in the details of this boasting, lying, pitiful man as only a master can. To match it, Portman gives one of his finest performances, mingling extreme sensitivity with broad strength. This is as good a performance as England can show.'

Guy Hamilton, director of Eric's previous film *The Colditz Story* spoke of *Separate Tables*: 'I will always remember the premiere. Eric played both leading parts: in the first act as a tough Labour leader and in the second act as a rather pathetic, dodgy, retired Major – parts played by Burt Lancaster and David Niven

Eric Portman and Phyllis Neillson-Terry in *Table by the Window* (© St James Theatre)

Eric as Major Pollock in *Table Number Seven* (© St James Theatre)

TABLE BY THE WINDOW

The first of two complementary plays by Terence Rattigan, presented by Stephen Mitchell, directed by Peter Glenville with decor by Michael Weight, and set in the Beauregard, a private hotel near Bournemouth

ERIC PORTMAN as Mr. Malcolm, the fallen Socialist politician. In *His Excellency*, a few years ago, he played a risen Socialist politician, and this role might be called the reverse side of the same penny; a man of brilliant intellect led to disaster by his physical desires and rough temper.

Eric as John Malcolm in *Table by the Window* (© St James Theatre)

in the subsequent film version. It was a typical example of his great versatility. I have nothing but fond memories of a talented and generous gentleman.'

In April 1954, while Eric Portman was achieving success in Rattigan's double-bill, the Grand Theatre, in Halifax, where he saw his first play as a young boy, was in dire straits. Audience numbers were dwindling, the theatre was losing money fast and the committee thought it would have to close. It did so on May 26th of that year, but thanks to a gift of £100 from Eric, it re-opened that July.

But two years previously, Eric had also stepped in to help the Grand Theatre and it was reported in the *Halifax Courier and Guardian* on 24th May 1952, how Eric commented that people were generally becoming more conscious of the value and quality of plays presented. One of the objects of the Club would be to choose plays that the audience would appreciate, then perform them at the Grand Theatre. Mr Eric Rothwell from the Club remarked that the theatre was not receiving the sort of support it ought to do, adding that only by supporting the theatre, would the public benefit from raising the standard of the plays and maybe perform plays by not so well-known authors.

But two years later, the theatre was in financial trouble again, so Eric Portman suggested that the Club should try to buy the Grand Theatre.

Eric Portman in Halifax

Eric Portman, the Halifax-born star of stage and screen, chats with Mr. J. Wood, secretary of Black Dyke Band, at the "Halifax Presents . . ." show at the Grand Theatre.

Eric and members of the Black Dyke Mills Band, performing at the fundraising stage show *Halifax Presents* (Courtesy of the Halifax Courier Ltd)

150

He took time out to visit the members, saying: 'Surely there are six persons or firms prepared to give £1,000 each?' he told the Grand Theatre committee. 'I know the Club has £1,000 in the kitty. That should be enough to start with – even if only as a mortgage. At Derby, the Playhouse was burnt out recently. We called a meeting and at once enormous sums of money were promised – and Halifax is wealthier than Derby. It would be a short-sighted policy to let the Grand go. The theatre could still be saved if Halifax people rally round. It would be a great loss to them and a terrible tragedy if it had to close.'

The Daily Herald later dubbed Eric 'The Fairy Godfather', because he was to help the theatre on four occasions. The first was the gift of £100, making it possible to re-open under the management of the newly formed Halifax Repertory Club in 1954, which was described as '…a voluntary band of enthusiastic people from all walks of life,' of which Eric was appointed President.

And his second 'gift' was the idea to stage a concert called 'Halifax Presents' – a variety show organised jointly by Eric Portman and Halifax actor Ivor Burgoyne, with the aim of providing funds for the newly formed Halifax Repertory Club.

The event attracted a full house, and at least three hundred people had to be turned away. The programme included dance, drama, comedy and music, with an appearance by the Black Dyke Mills Band. Jean Richardson, who lives not far from me, remembers being part of a dance troupe as a young girl and performing in the show.

Theatre programme for stage show
Halifax Presents

Eric and an unknown colleague outside the Grand Theatre, Halifax (source unknown)

She recalled her memory of Eric Portman's entrance onto the stage – not from the wings – but on a lift which came up through the trapdoor!

Eric Portman received a huge round of applause, started with a performance piece, under the title 'All The World's A Stage,' where he was assisted by various people including his nephews John and Michael Portman.

'What a beautiful theatre!' he told the audience. 'You must not let it go, this little theatre that I loved so long ago. Shakespeare, East Lynne, whatever the play, the living theatre shall not die!'

He said he was '…tremendously impressed by the talent of youth clubs.' The most notable thing about the entertainment was the remarkable way in which the amateurs had rallied to help the professionals. He particularly paid tribute to the Halifax Thespians who staged amateur productions, saying that there was not such an organisation in Halifax in his day. Although this was a confusing statement in itself

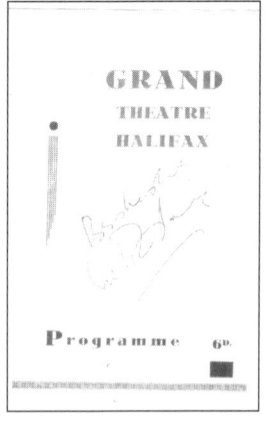

Eric's autograph on the *Halifax Presents* theatre programme

because both he and Wilfred Pickles were in the King Cross Amateur Dramatic Society and had also appeared in other local acting groups, such as the Halifax Light Opera Society.

On the subject of raising money for the Halifax Repertory Club, he said: 'I cannot think tonight that there is anyone against such an idea in this remarkable theatre. Play-acting is as exciting there, as in London or anywhere else.'

Mrs C. Grenshaw, Chairman of the new Repertory Club, paid tribute to Eric Portman and Ivor Burgoyne. Eric, particularly, who had spent a good deal of time, travelling the 400-mile round trip from London to Halifax and back, during the night, to keep in touch with them, and to help organise the event, despite his busy schedule in performing *Separate Tables* in the capital.

Eric told the *Courier & Guardian* that the Grand was ideal structurally and was capable of being made into an 'attractive rendezvous' for people, with a café included. One thing he was especially interested in was to recapture the theatre's atmosphere of former days. He thought the complaint that the Grand was situated at the wrong end of town was complete nonsense. Given the production of simple, straightforward plays, he felt that the Grand would succeed again. However, he did add that they must avoid bad plays.

Eric Portman and the management committee at Grand Theatre, Halifax. Former theatre manager Donald Walker is on the left
(Courtesy of the Halifax Courier Ltd)

Eric Moorcroft, publicity officer of the Club, later wrote that this new venue was looked upon as one of the best in the North of England for its high standard of plays and performance. 'Not that the audiences showed up in full strength,' he wrote, 'but the enterprise did just tick over.'

'Ticking over', however, was not enough to keep a theatre running keeping a troupe of actors in employment on an indefinite basis, so another plan was required to secure more long-term sustainability, and it came about the following year.

Donald Walker answered my media appeal and told how he obtained his first professional post as Theatre Director of the Grand, in 1955. He writes: 'The financial situation was very unstable. The actors were on minimum salaries and each production was staged on a shoestring, limping from week to week with an enthusiastic, loyal following but not enough seats filled to guarantee a solid future. As Spring turned into Summer and with a strengthening of the acting standard, business started to pick up, though not sufficiently for any complacency. During the thankfully mild Autumn, business remained fairly constant, crowned by a very successful pantomime of *Aladdin* which at last showed a little profit to carry forward into the New Year. An approach to the town council resulted in a one-off grant of £500 which made it possible to buy some second-hand scenery and engage a scenic artist. No longer did we need to hire scenery, which was sometimes quite unsuitable, on a weekly basis from Bradford. The standard of production improved immediately and everything seemed to be coming into place at last.'

'There was just one thing we could not control – the weather. Keen frost and then snow, before January was out: the old boiler did its best to provide a little heat in the building but outside it was freezing and people understandably stayed at home. We were back to square one: minus one.

After a month or so of diminishing houses, I wrote, in desperation, to Halifax's most successful progeny – Eric Portman. He was appearing at that time in the original production of Terence Rattigan's play *Separate Tables* at the St James' Theatre in London. His reply came by return of post including a personal cheque for £100 to help with that week's salaries.'

This was Eric's third gift – along with the advice: 'The way to make money is to put on popular plays every year. Give the people what they want – five farces and four strong melodramas.'

He later commented to the press '…it is all very well for the 'old faithfuls' helping the club again but it has been the lower-income folk who have kept the Grand open. Where are the people with money in Halifax? They should be in the theatre seats, helping as these others have done. Surely large local firms could help?'

Eric Moorcroft warned that: '…the loss of repertory to any town meant the loss of a training school for actors….audiences do not want TV thrust down their throats; they want individuality.' He felt that although TV had taken a strong part in people's lives he was convinced that this new medium was only a temporary menace!!!

By January 1956, there was still a major lack of finance, and so Eric's brother, Leslie, who ran the family business and was one of the enthusiastic members of the Repertory Club, decided to be 'cheeky' and asked what seemed impossible. Would Eric Portman come to do a one-night show?

At the time, Eric had a heavy schedule. Not only was he performing in *Separate Tables* in London, but was also working on a new film called *Child in the House*. And yet such was his commitment to preserving the provincial repertory theatre tradition, and also the theatre where he had seen his first play, that he told Donald Walker to organise a mass meeting at the Grand. The following Sunday, he travelled up from London to speak to the Club's members. The local press had given the event great publicity and the stalls in the auditorium were very nearly full. Eric arrived just an hour before the meeting, saying that he could only stay for four hours before heading back to London.

In answer to his brother's suggestion, Eric told the Repertory Club and the press that he was prepared to appear with a West End leading lady, in a play of his own choice on a Sunday evening at the Grand Theatre. He would travel from London on three consecutive Sundays – two for rehearsals and one for a performance. And this would turn out to be the Fairy Godfather's fourth gift to the theatre.

He said: 'This would be very hard work and would involve rehearsals in the train with my leading lady. But I am prepared to do anything possible to prevent the Grand closing down.'

Donald Walker recalls: 'Eric gave a most stirring speech before sending us to the prop room to bring any receptacle we could find, (the members didn't have proper collection trays so they grabbed what they could, including aspidistra pots, a coal scuttle and a shopping basket!) and these were circulated through the audience to raise a Fighting Fund to help us carry on. Then members of the club committee and cast went among the 350 members sat in the auditorium

Plan by Eric Portman to keep Halifax theatre open

ERIC PORTMAN, the Halifax-born stage and screen actor, rushed from London yesterday to make a "stay open" appeal on behalf of the Halifax Grand Theatre.

As a boy he saw the famous stage stars from a seat in the gallery and grew up to become himself recognised as one of the country's leading actors.

He is president of the Halifax Repertory Theatre Club—the company now facing a closure threat for the second time in a year.

£100 GIFT

So determined was Mr. Portman that Halifax's last "straight" theatre should stay on the map that he handed the club chairman, Mr. Leonard Kendall, a cheque for £100.

More than 350 members of the club in the theatre followed his

Eric's plan to save the Grand Theatre, Halifax (Courtesy of the Halifax Courier Ltd)

156

Eric with brother Leslie and sister-in-law Alice (© Yorkshire Observer)

and collected £170 in £1 notes and 10 shilling pieces.'

Soon afterwards, Eric left the theatre to catch the night train back to London. He must have known that his original plan of travelling by train with an actress from London to Halifax on three consecutive Sundays, was not the most practical arrangement, and so on Tuesday 21st February 1956, he telephoned his brother Leslie to say he had come up with a better idea and then visited Halifax again to announce it to the Club members and the Press, who had gathered together again in the Grand Theatre.

When Eric arrived, he revealed his new plan: to bring the whole cast and crew of *Separate Tables* to Halifax to perform at the Grand for one night only.

The audience were astounded.

Eric Moorcroft pointed out that for the whole cast of a West End play to be transferred 'en bloc' just for one night's performance must have been something of a record – unknown in theatre history.

So many preparations had to be made. First of all, full written permission had to be sought from the producers of the play – the management of the Royal St James' Theatre. Terence Rattigan had to be contacted overseas for his blessing – which he readily gave. Phone calls were made each night from Halifax to London and to Eric Portman's flat after each night's performance. Moorcroft sat through many long phone calls discussing the courtesies of billing acknowledgements and so on. Copies of bill matter and programme layouts had to be sent to London for sanction.

Train journeys were then made by the stage manager Harry Speed, scenic artist Maurice Davis, and theatre director Donald Walker, measuring the sets, planning the furniture, photos made of the stage plans, with exact replicas of the London sets reproduced. John Crossleys, the Halifax-based local textile manufacturers, made exact copies of the on-stage carpets with the backstage also fully carpeted to deaden all noise behind the scenes.

The stage manager of the Grand Theatre, Harry Speed, had a hectic weekend because immediately after the Repertory Club's performance of *The Shining Hour* finished on Saturday night, he and his staff set to work dismantling the set, and erecting the new one for *Separate Tables*. They worked through until 4.30am in the morning and were back on the job again at 9am.

Donald Walker says: 'The show itself was organised backstage by Joan Preston, the stage manager and company manager for the London production. She arrived early on Sunday morning to oversee the acquisition of all furniture and props, organise the food for the dining room scenes, conduct the lighting rehearsal in the afternoon and to instruct our stage management team in their duties.'

The theatre was a complete sell-out, days before the big night. Every national paper was represented and theatre critics from London came north to this provincial theatre for this big event. As the Grand Theatre's publicity officer, Moorcroft had the task of keeping them all informed, with his telephone constantly ringing with those checking dates and times.

Ron Winn, who was then honorary musical adviser to the Grand Theatre, gathered his team of musicians to play the incidental music. Lighting was exact – spots, etc, all carefully planned. The cast was amazed at the complete authenticity of the effect. Moorcroft recalled: 'The crunch came when we had to engage the stage crew from Leeds Grand Theatre, as the Union demanded. It was an expense we had not envisaged.'

It was decided that in order to fund the Grand Theatre for the foreseeable future, West End ticket prices of between five shillings and three guineas were charged for each seat and, in addition, that only members of the Repertory Club would be allowed in for the big night, which resulted in an extra 2,000 members signing up with annual subscriptions, meaning that the theatre was safe once again.

Eric Portman paid all the expenses for the cast – at a total of £200 – but he wouldn't talk about that. 'As long as we managed to save rep in Halifax and keep the theatre going, it doesn't matter. The whole experience is an absorbing one for me. It was here I had my first glimpse of the theatre as a seven-year-old boy. It was a melodrama called *A London Actress*. I was thrilled.'

Eric Portman, his co-star Margaret Leighton and eighteen other members of the company, including stage management and wardrobe department, all gave up their day off, and worked without pay, to travel the 400-mile round trip to Halifax.

Eric Portman and Margaret Leighton in *Separate Tables* (© the former St James Theatre, London)

Says Donald Walker: 'The cast and crew gave their scheduled matinee and evening performances at the St James Theatre in London on the Saturday (as the Halifax Repertory Club did at the Grand Theatre, Halifax) and travelled up to Leeds on the Sunday morning to check into the Queens Hotel. I think the actors arrived at the Grand Theatre at about 5pm on the

Sunday and, after settling into their dressing rooms, came up on stage to 'walk' the set.

Margaret Leighton told a journalist: 'We all owe so much to repertory. The least we can do is to help it when it needs us. I feel tremendously excited, because we're helping Eric's hometown.' Eric Portman commented: 'Halifax keeps its character. Halifax has got something which a great many towns and cities don't understand. I hope I will never lose my touch with the town.'

Donald Walker recalls that when the cast saw the copied set, they felt as if they were playing, as usual, at the St James Theatre, but they were not exact replicas. He says: 'The London production had been mounted on a revolving stage, alternating between the lounge and dining room settings. Yet this was not possible on the Halifax stage, so two separate sets had to be constructed from our small stock of recently acquired scenery, thus copying, as far as possible the original designs. This involved the stage staff in four strike-and-reset scene changes, with only the back wall of the lounge set remaining throughout the whole performance. However, the staircase on the set was a little narrower than the original in London, and I remember the actress Phyllis Neilson-Terry walking down the steps, explaining to the rest of the cast: "Oh, it's quite easy; you just have to come down slightly sideways – like a crab." So then we all had a cup of tea, before the cast returned to their dressing rooms to prepare for that extraordinary show.

Cartoon of Eric as Major Pollock in *Separate Tables* (source unknown)

Says Donald: 'The news had spread beyond the Halifax boundary and the theatre was packed. Some local people were upset that they were unable to afford the inflated ticket prices but most loyal supporters understood that this was to save their theatre.'

The *Daily Herald* reported that, prior to the show, an old man stood in the wings and cried. He was Bobby Spence, stage doorkeeper and usher, saying that he could remember Eric as a young lad, playing his first season in repertory at the former Theatre Royal, Halifax.

A conversation occurred in broad Yorkshire between Eric and Bobby.

'Staying to see the show, Bobby?'

'Nay, ah'd miss the bus.'

'Treat thisen to a taxi. Nay lad, I'll treat thee to a taxi.'

Also attending that night and seated in the Orchestra stalls were Margaret Rutherford and Robert Morley who were performing in a show at the Grand Theatre, in Leeds, (Morley had donated £50 to the Halifax Repertory Club) and Laurence Harvey who travelled to the theatre with Miss Leighton. Also present were Eric's brothers 'Our Cliff' and 'Our Leslie', although no mention was made of his sister Winifred.

As the audience settled into their seats that night, no doubt they would have opened the souvenir theatre programme detailing the evening's performance and read the foreword by Eric Moorcroft:

<u>Our Eric</u>

'Eric has come home. His beloved theatre must NOT close. He's here to keep it open.'

'Eric is now acknowledged as one of our leading actors but his success has not altered him – his kindness, generosity and forbearing are still there. He always will be "Our Eric".'

FROM LONDON SHOW TO STRUGGLING, THE STARS HELP TO S[AVE]

Eric Portman even felt nervous

From KENNETH YATES : HALIFAX, Sunday.

FOR a few hours a little bit of West End glamour came to Northgate here tonight. And Halifax folk loved it. They sometimes laughed in the wrong place and made Eric Portman—the local boy who made good—nervous. But who cared?

For a night they paid West End prices for a London play in the Grand Theatre—and really enjoyed paying out.

Mr. Portman — his brother Leslie, a Halifax tailor, was at the theatre too—brought the play Separate Tables, with its star-studded West End cast, to Halifax to raise money to save the 76-year-old theatre from going bankrupt.

With Margaret Leighton as his co-star and 18 other members of the company from St. James's Theatre he arrived from London.

All offered to give up their day off to go with him on the 400-mile round trip to the provinces to save repertory in this Yorkshire mill town.

He paid expenses

When they saw the audience —900-strong — they were so delighted they had. For most of them it was the first time they had played rep. in Halifax. Only Mr. Portman had appeared in plays there before. "And I was not as nervous then as I am now," he said.

To the audience who paid from 5s. to three guineas for tickets he was still "Our Eric" —the local boy who first went with his mother and father to the theatre when he was seven, long before acting got into his blood. Later he played in rep. in Halifax—at the Theatre Royal, not the Grand—for £20 a week.

Mr. Portman paid all expenses for the cast himself. It cost him £200. But he wouldn't talk about that. "As long as we managed to save rep. in Halifax and keep the theatre going it doesn't matter."

top and middle left:

The cast of *Separate Tables* arrive at the Grand Theatre, Halifax (Courtesy of the Halifax Courier Ltd)

All the tension of a West End opening night

LONDON CAST IN ONE-NIGHT SHOW IN HALIFAX

Left: Autograph hunters are ready for Margaret Leighton, Eric Portman's co-star, as she arrives at the theatre. Below: Crowds surge around the stage door of Halifax's Grand Theatre as the West End cast of "Separate Tables" arrives. Eric Portman is seen leaving the motor-coach.

Crowds surge around Grand Theatre stage door

above: Reporting Eric's appearance in the Halifax production of *Separate Tables* left: The cast of *Separate Tables* arrives in Halifax (Both courtesy of the Halifax Courier Ltd)

'We thank you, Eric, and these wonderful artistes who have travelled here tonight and have given their services free to keep your Theatre open. Thank you for coming home to us Eric. You are always welcome.'

In his article, 'Never A Night So Grand', (published over twenty years later in the *Halifax Courier* on March 19th 1976): Eric Moorcroft recounted how the cast were full of 'opening night nerves', despite the fact that they had been performing *Separate Tables* to packed houses in London for the previous eighteen months. One of the cast, Basil Henson said: 'We're all as nervous as kittens. It's very exciting.' Even Eric Portman, despite his decades of experience on the stage said that he felt even more nervous than he had ever before.

When the play began, and the curtain went up to a huge round of applause, Eric was struck silent for a moment, later admitting to Moorcroft how it was the first time he had 'dried' (forgotten his lines) on an entrance.

The cost of the company's accommodation at the Queen's Hotel, in Leeds was borne entirely by Eric Portman and the only charges he made upon Halifax was for a bottle of his favourite spirits to be on his dressing-room table. Eric Moorcroft recalled seeing Laurence Harvey, Margaret Leighton, Robert Morley, Violet Fairbrother, Margaret Rutherford and Jimmy Thompson, (also from Halifax).

He wrote: 'All these celebrities had come to pay tribute to Eric Portman for a fine gesture in the home town of which he was always proud. I was proud to have been connected to that brilliant night, a night to remember all one's life. Halifax turned out in fine style – the dressing of the audience compared with that of a Royal Command Performance.'

After the fall of the curtain, Eric took '…curtain call after curtain call and was cheered by a capacity audience.' He told them: 'It is a remarkable evening. Every member of our company has been happy to do this. But the rest of the company deserves more credit than I do. I have a duty to come here – they have the pleasure.'

Then he read out a telegram he received from the writer of the play, which read: 'Regret I cannot be with you tonight. Best wishes for the future – Terence Rattigan.' Then Eric introduced members of the Halifax Repertory Theatre Club cast. He said: 'These are the people who are going to keep the Grand Theatre going for some time.'

Eric signing autographs at the Grand Theatre, Halifax
(Both courtesy of the Halifax Courier Ltd)

Moorcroft continued: 'In a speech, he asked for the loyal support of Halifax in keeping the Grand alive, but the days of the Grand became numbered, as in so many other theatres. This lovely old place, shabby though it was, had the finest acoustics and was designed by Frank Matcham, whose other buildings, such as the London Palladium, and the Grand Theatre in Blackpool, were monuments.'

Donald Walker says: 'After the show, the cast returned to the Queen's Hotel in Leeds, then returned to London on the Monday, in time to play their usual evening performance that evening. It had no doubt been a tiring weekend for the older members of the company.'

After the show, the last to leave the theatre was old Bobby Spence who had – after all – stayed to see the play. 'Don't worry about me,' he told a journalist. 'I've got a taxi.'

The audience left the theatre but for the stage crew, the night had only just begun. The stage manager Maurice Speed and his stage crew worked all night again to dismantle the set, and create a new set for the next play by the Repertory Club – *French Without Tears* – another play by Terence Rattigan.

Moorcroft recalled: 'At the conclusion of the show, Eric Portman invited my wife and me to a party at his hotel in Leeds. In spite of a heavy day, he was still full of energy; we less so.'

'The following morning the national press paid tribute to Eric Portman's effort and a fine performance on stage and, once again, the *Separate Tables* stars were playing to full houses in London on the Monday evening – just as though they had enjoyed a day's rest. Will Halifax ever again see the like?'

'Eric Portman was without doubt a most popular man in the theatre. I had letters from him of appreciation for my part in that gala occasion. Before his departure that night, he made gifts to many of the backroom workers. The cost that day must have been heavy upon his purse, but he enjoyed giving as he enjoyed being kind to all who came his way.'

Many years later, local actress Sybil Holroyd remembered the night: 'The evening was historic and long to be remembered by all present. I was a member of the committee which tried to keep the Grand Theatre alive and that exciting evening had a sequel for me. After the show, Eric Portman asked me to go to London the next day and see the show again at the St James' Theatre, where he would see that a seat was reserved for me. This I duly did and, in his dressing room afterwards, the young couple in the play came in (the man was Basil Henson) carrying a large bottle of champagne as a thank-you present for Eric who said: 'I just don't understand. I thought everyone was doing me a favour by coming to Halifax, but they all keep thanking me!' The couple replied: "But it was the most exciting weekend we ever had! It felt quite flat to be back at the St James's tonight!" Then Eric rounded everything off by taking me out to supper at the Caprice, which was a lovely finish to two real red-letter evenings.'

Donald Walker says: 'As for the Grand, there was enough money in the bank to see us safely through the rest of the cold weather and the publicity of the great event certainly had a beneficial effect on box office takings thereafter. Sadly though, only a few months later and due to many years of neglected maintenance, part of the plaster ceiling above the auditorium fell in – luckily, after the audience had left for the night. The building was immediately condemned for public use – and so ended a great enterprise.'

'This incident does, I believe, show a side of Eric's generous nature, as well as being a bit of theatre history when a West End production came to the aid of a small, ailing provincial rep.'

As an interesting footnote, a letter appeared in the *Halifax Courier* from local resident Mrs Mildred Barraclough, referring to a previous article about the actor.

She writes: 'I agree that Eric Portman was the most famous film star (and stage star) that Halifax has produced, and I well remember Matthew Portman's shop in the old Arcade Royale. …My husband and I are great theatre fans. We went to see (Eric) in London in Terence Rattigan's *Separate Tables* which was the Number One show at that time. Eric Portman played two totally different parts in the plays which made up *Separate Tables*, with no extravagant make-up, and it was hard to believe it was the same person. We had the pleasure of meeting him in his dressing room afterwards. I told him how glad I was that he had got his name in lights at last, and he said, very realistically: "They could go out tonight!" (Courtesy of Halifax Courier Ltd)

CHAPTER 9

A TIPPLE TOO FAR

Eric appeared in several TV productions, presumably made during breaks of the two-year British tour of *Separate Tables*, one of which was for the *Theatre Royal* series, playing the title role in *Mr Betts Runs Away*. A journalist remarked that he thought Eric had abandoned filmmaking altogether, as he had been concentrating on theatre work, and Eric replied: 'Yes, I suppose I haven't made as many films as I might have, but then I've had such wonderful luck in the theatre; four out of the last five plays I've appeared in have run for more than a year. *Separate Tables* has been running for two years, of course. Let's say the stage parts offered me were too tempting to resist. Really, I want to do plays and films if I can. It's nice to have two strings to one's bow.'

Eric's next film was *Child in the House* released in 1955, and made the previous year during his attempts to save the Grand Theatre from closure. Directed by Cy Endfield, this is a British drama which tells the story of a girl who struggles to cope with her uncaring relatives. Based on a novel by Janet McNeill, it starred Phyllis Calvert, Stanley Baker, Dora Bryan, Victor Maddern, Joan Hickson (who would later play TV's *Miss Marple*), and had smaller parts for Alfie Bass and Maggie Smith.

Quite how Eric found the time to appear in the film while he was appearing in *Separate Tables* is anyone's guess, but as the British tour of the play was coming to an end, and arrangements were being made to take it on tour of America, Eric, who liked to keep busy, was looking for more work.

One such acting job was another long-forgotten TV production called *The Last Reunion*, followed by a radio play for the BBC. Entitled *The Case of Private Hamp* it was produced in the Home Service on Monday October 1st, with the leading roles played by Eric Portman and Noel Johnson (who played the title character in the radio series: *Dick Barton: Special Agent*). Set during the First World War, *The Case of Private Hamp* is a grim, gripping account of a soldier's sudden inability to stand any more fighting. Hamp deserts and is court-martialled on the most serious charge a soldier can face and much of the play concerns the compelling court-martial proceedings and the efforts of Lieutenant Hargreaves, Hamp's commander, to save him. Eric played Hargreaves and Noel Johnson played the simple Lancashire soldier who broke and ran.

Eric photographed by the *Radio Times* for some of his work at BBC TV (Courtesy of the Radio Times)

Margaret Medawar tells me: 'My sister and I saw (Eric) at the opening of Yorkshire Television Centre in Leeds and he was at the Town Hall there. My sister tried to see him by going round the back of the Hall but we only saw the actress Janette Scott (who was aged about sixteen at the time) and we got her autograph before a policeman asked us to leave. He promised to get Eric

Portman's autograph and post it to us. Needless to say, that never happened!'

The same year he also appeared in another TV production called *A Double Life*, and one other for the Theatre Royal TV series, entitled *The Case of Dr Crippen*, in which he portrayed the notorious killer. Soon after, yet another opportunity arose for a film. A press report dated 16th June 1956, read: 'A Yorkshireman to play a Yorkshireman.' It stated how filming was under way at the Associated British Studios at Elstree, of a musical version of J. B. Priestley's play *The Good Companions*. Eric had been cast as Jess Oakroyd, 'that big-hearted son of "Bruddesford", and the report said that 'Eric Portman should be the right man for the role.'

Eric later said: 'It was only a matter of luck that I was able to take on the Jess Oakroyd part in *The Good Companions* – the film happened to be made between the end of the (British) run (of *Separate Tables*) at St James's and my departure for New York. However, I'm glad I didn't miss the opportunity – being a Yorkshireman myself the idea of playing Jess appealed to me very much.'

A journalist remarked that Eric's ability to 'turn on' a Yorkshire accent had proved useful.

'It certainly has,' agreed the actor. 'As a matter of fact, the people at Elstree studios offered me the Jess Oakroyd part because they remembered me as the Yorkshire foreman in the wartime munitions film, *Millions Like Us*. One of my favourite parts was that of the Yorkshire labour-leader in *His Excellency*. And through *Separate Tables* – which is really two plays – I give a suave, cultured accent to one of the characters I portray, a sophisticated type – to the other, a rough sort of chap, I give a Yorkshire accent again.'

The film also starred Celia Johnson, Hugh Griffith, Joyce Grenfell and Shirley Anne Field, and was directed and co-produced by J. Lee Thompson.

Shirley Anne Field told Tony Earnshaw: 'I filmed with Eric Portman for months on *The Good Companions* – I was about 17 and played 'The Three

Graces.' You can't imagine what it was like to be a young girl in the film industry. I've met a lot of stars who are horrid, but all the big people on *The Good Companions* were extraordinary. Everybody you can name was in that film: Celia Johnson, Hugh Griffith, Janette Scott, Thora Hird…some great classical British actors. And Eric was wonderful – one of the kindest people I've ever come across. He'd always give up his chair for me – he had a named chair and I didn't, of course, because I was really just a glorified extra – so he'd make sure I had a seat. He used to tell me about Marilyn Monroe and how common she'd been when he had met her. He said: "She doesn't have a nose like you, darling." He was a great friend to me. And of course I learned a lot from him.'

As Eric was about to set sail for the States for the continuing run of *Separate Tables*, he was interviewed again by the journalist R. Quilter Vincent. Eric said he had a pleasant surprise when he realised he would be sailing on September the thirteenth – as this was his lucky number (probably because it was his birthday) '…so it augurs well for my trip that it begins on that date.'

The American tour of *Separate Tables* was arranged for a provisional duration of six months, which was a conservative estimate. Eric told a journalist that a play may be a sensation in one country but may not work in another, although Americans who had seen the play in London told him they had loved it. It was to be given a trial run in places like Boston and then, if successful, it would play on Broadway in New York for a full six months run, up until June 1956. Eric pointed out that it would have to come off for two months because 'New York will be having its usual heatwave', but that it may then continue after that. He thought that he may look for more work in the US during the summer break, and may even try Hollywood.

He said: "If I were offered something really exciting I might go. I went to Hollywood before the war, you know, but didn't care much for it then. It would be different now, of course. I'm better known and consequently I'd feel more at ease, more confident. But even if I don't make a film, I dare say there'll be offers to make television appearances of one sort or another.'

Eric went with the production of *Separate Tables* to the Music Box Theatre in New York in October 1956 and toured America with it until January 1958. While in New York, a journalist wrote of the realism that Eric brought to his role, and Eric told him he believed that being an actor required no particular brains. 'I keep hearing about Method. I don't know if there's a method in acting at all. To me, it's quite incredible – going into a room to learn to act. It's like people who go to learn to have a personality.'

Around this time, according to a clipping from the *New York Times*, Eric was involved a crash between a car and the taxi he was travelling in, in New York. He and the taxi driver were both treated in hospital for lacerations and contusions of the face and chest but were not detained. I also heard from John Ferguson, one of Eric's neighbours, that Harry McLarnon, the actor's secretary, was murdered while the play was touring New York, but unfortunately, I have been unable to discover any further information on the matter.

Although *Separate Tables* completed its run, it did not see the actor slow down in his workload. He appeared in two TV productions: the long-forgotten *A Double Life* and *A Tale of Two Cities*, the latter in which he played the character Sydney Carlton. In May 1958, he played Mr Rochester in *Jane Eyre* at the Belasco Theatre, which then transferred to the Helen Hayes Theatre that October. Still at that theatre he took on the part of Cornelius Melody in *A Touch of the Poet* by Eugene O'Neill, opening at the Helen Hayes Theatre, which also featured Helen Hayes herself and Kim Stanley. Brooks Atkinson wrote: 'The acting of Miss Hayes, Miss Stanley and Mr Portman brought a random script vigorously alive.'

The journalist William Glover interviewed Eric in New York on 19th October 1958 and wrote: 'All out and fearless' is how Eric Portman describes his work in

A Touch of the Poet by Eugene O'Neill. He plays a vain, tormented and finally crushed Irishman in New England in 1828.'

Eric told him: 'It is a hell'u'va difficult part. But what's so tremendous about it, is that it grows and you can grow in it. It demands almost the physically impossible. As for the interpretation (of the role), it is tremendous bravura, of course. It demands the inherent nervous energy that I am. Bravura is second nature to a Yorkshireman – the large voice, the big gestures.'

'I believe American audiences do like this type of acting, perhaps for a change. Your last one I think was John Barrymore. Now there seems to be room for a few of us again.'

'I can sympathise with (my character). He was a soldier who should have been killed in heroic battle. Like so many people in war, he was a tragic figure who lived too long.'

The journalist observed how Eric: '…tumbles his thoughts out in a clipped, almost breathless succession.'

'I know we English actors talk too fast for audiences here,' Eric said, regarding the comment of some critics that snatches of his speeches in *A Touch of the Poet*, cannot be caught by listeners. 'I am working on that right now, slowing down, part of the job of getting the inner details done. Every day, I remind myself.'

The journalist recounted how Eric previously played 'the boy' in O'Neill's play *Desire Under The Elms* and felt considerable trepidation when producer Robert Whitehead eyed him for the assignment some eighteen months previously, during his success in *Separate Tables*. After that, Whitehead took Eric to meet O'Neill's widow, who inscribed a copy of the play to him. Later, the star insisted on a full-cast reading.

Eric said: 'When that was done, I felt sure for the first time that I could take a shot at it. It has a false simplicity – (it) seems almost banal when you read it. But something mysterious happens – I don't know what – when it is delivered and profoundly affects an audience. That's true, of course, of so much of O'Neill.'

The journalist asked him how he felt about doing a play which runs for a long time. Contradicting exactly what he had said in previous interviews, he commented: 'I'm one of those that doesn't mind staying a long time with one play. I think the opposite tendency of so many actors today is a little unfortunate. Always wanting to jump about and try something different. Sheer versatility, you know, isn't the answer to everything.'

The play was still running by 20th March 1959, when a newspaper reported how Kim Stanley had resigned, being critical of one of her co-stars – Eric Portman.

A week later, the same newspaper announced a second resignation, of an actress who had reportedly 'walked out in a huff.' Nancy Malone, Ms Stanley's 24-year-old understudy who took over the role, says her complaint is 'pride linked with money,' and handed in her two weeks' notice. As an understudy, Miss Malone got $150 dollars a week, plus $35 whenever she appeared on stage when Miss Stanley was ill. She was offered $450 on taking over permanently – but demanded $500. Producer Robert Whithead turned down her demand.

But why had the original star, Kim Stanley, resigned?

Irene Holloway, who befriended Eric Portman after she saw him in *The Browning Version* may provide a clue. She tells me that while Eric was in America '..his drinking got out of control, when he would drink before and during a performance – something he never did (in Britain). His leading lady Kim Stanley didn't like him, for after a few drinks he could become very insulting, as he was when he met (the actress) Tallulah Bankhead in a park when he reduced her to tears. He would wake up next morning, full of remorse and wondering what he could do to make amends – but he couldn't.'

Despite the arguments and resignations, the play still ran until October 1959, and Eric was next seen on American TV, playing Fagin in a CBS version of

Oliver Twist, which also featured fellow English actor Robert Morley as Mr Brownlow. A report dated 27th November 1959 declared that: 'Sensitive viewers...need have no fears. Portman intends to play the old boy without accent – even the one Dickens gave him.'

Eric said: 'I shan't play him as a dirty greasy crook either. My make-up will make me look like a vaguely saintly Rasputin – but he could do anything. There will be no suggestion of – no caricature of – any race.'

Though one reviewer of the screening said: 'Eric Portman was an impressive Fagin physically, but I had trouble understanding him – a common complaint against Portman who simply won't take it seriously,' no doubt referring to the critics of his performance in O'Neill's play when he reportedly talked too fast for American audiences.

I was contacted by a 91-year-old gentleman, who saw my appeal for information in his local newspaper. Mr F. Forbes worked as an electrician and stage-hand at the Salisbury Theatre in Wiltshire. Here, he befriended Eric Portman during a theatrical tour. As it was such a long time ago, Mr Forbes could not recall the length of the stay at Salisbury, nor the name of the play, though it may well have been *A Touch of the Poet*, which begun in New York in 1958, then transferred to England the following year. Mr Forbes described Eric as someone who largely kept to himself and did not appear to be part of the showbiz crowd. But Mr Forbes's comments also substantiate what Irene Holloway was saying about the actor's drinking habits.

'Eric was very partial to gin,' Mr Forbes recalled. 'As an actor, he had a fantastic voice, and his performances were all the better for it, when he had had a few. I used to nip over to the Military Officer's Club across the road, and buy gin for him.'

He said that after the run at Salisbury, people at the theatre were expecting to get hand-outs from Eric – no doubt news of his generosity had spread – but the actor was having none of it. 'Eric was always kind to me, though' says Mr Forbes. 'And he also gave me a signed photograph which I still have.'

On yet one more transatlantic hop, Eric returned to New York to play the title role in *Flowering Cherry* by Robert Bolt which opened in October 1959. The plot centres around Jim Cherry, who works as a clerk in an insurance office, which he hates, but dreams of owning an orchard in Somerset. After an argument with his boss, he leaves the job, and his wife considers leaving him, as his rebellious attitude is now rubbing off on their children. In frustration with his lot, he has a stroke and dies, still dreaming of his orchard. This was based on Robert Bolt's own experience of working as a clerk in an insurance office, which he stuck for just a year, for he absolutely loathed the deadening work ethic and the tedium of the daily grind, brought on by his belief that he could do better, coupled with the frustrating lack of an opportunity to escape it. The theme, though not the plot, sounds much like other plays I have read, most notably *The Good and Faithful Servant* by Joe Orton and *A Memory of Two Mondays* by Arthur Miller – of people trapped in tedious or unsuitable employment, as Eric had previously referred to in one of his interviews.

Eric played the title role as Jim Cherry, with Wendy Hiller as his wife Isobel, and he was following on from a successful run from the previous year after Sir Ralph Richardson had played the character. In his book *The Lost Summer: The Heyday of the West End Theatre*, Charles Duff writes that theatre producer Frith Banbury considered Eric 'a fine actor of the very first rank,' rated below Olivier and Gielgud, only because he had played fewer of the classic drama texts than those two giants of the theatre. But Eric's drinking bouts were starting to affect his work, and Mr Duff writes: '…what no one associated with the enterprise then realised was that he had become an alcoholic.'

Amongst the cast was Dame Wendy Hiller, who said that Eric could not walk and talk at the same time, and at one rehearsal she phoned playwright Robert

Bolt and said: 'I can't bear it.' Later, she complained to the theatre management saying: 'It's a very long way for me to come just to act with an alcoholic.'

At one point, Eric insisted on having a drunken onstage discussion with Frith Banbury, and when someone enquired what Eric's performance had been like, Robert Bolt had answered 'Drunk!'

Although Eric was sober during a daytime dress-rehearsal he was described as 'paralytic' during the press conference, held two hours later for the American press. Banbury apologised the next morning and, after the opening night, Robert Bolt left New York by boat, to avoid the reviews. As he suspected, they were terrible and the play only ran to four performances.

One of Frith Banbury's colleagues told him: 'It is sad about Eric, but we have learned our lesson.'

I have seen it stated that Eric was still in the play when it was transferred to the Lyceum, in London, though the above report suggests this was unlikely.

CHAPTER 10

THE FINAL CURTAIN

By 1960, due to his stage success with *Separate Tables*, Eric had not made a film for cinematic release since *The Good Companions* four years previously, so after *Flowering Cherry* he signed up for another movie.

Released in May 1961 in the UK, and the following month in the US, *Naked Edge* was a thriller – a British-American co-production. Eric got third billing behind the two leads, Gary Cooper and Deborah Kerr and, as it turned out, it was Cooper's last film.

Directed by Michael Anderson for United Artists, the movie was shot in London and Elstree Studios in Hertfordshire. Apart from Cooper, Kerr and Eric, the film also features Hermione Gingold, Michael Wilding, Ray McAnally, Wilfred Lawson, Joyce Carey and Peter Cushing.

The plot involves a businessman who is stabbed to death when a mailbag of money is stolen from an office one night, when the only two people present are the employees Donald Heath and George Radcliffe. Heath is convicted, partly on Radcliffe's testimony, but Radcliffe's wife, Martha, suspects her husband is guilty of the crime.

Months later, the mailbag is found and the Radcliffes receive a letter which was in the bag. The letter is a blackmail threat from Jeremy Gray, (played by Eric), accusing George of the crime.

As the plot unfolds, there are many clues to pointing to Radcliffe as the guilty party, and Gray tells Martha that he was witness to the crime and that her husband is indeed guilty. This is a film with a mystery central to the plot, so I won't continue the description and spoil the surprise just in case you are planning to watch the movie!

The director Michael Anderson told Tony Earnshaw how Eric '…had quite a spectacular part, in a sense, because he was the star of the end of the movie. He wasn't at all intimidated by Gary Cooper; he was his own man and a star in his own right. Their acting styles were different but the roles were so different that it was merely a question of character rather than choice. Eric developed his character in conjunction with myself and in consultation with 'Coop'. He was chosen because he was an icon – the actor playing that part had to be up to the standard that the movie was requiring. So it was a choice and he was the right choice. He and Coop got on very well. I wish I'd worked with Eric more and had known him better, because he was just splendid to work with.'

From the reports of Eric's drinking habits, they seemed limited entirely to theatre work. Perhaps it was live performances which were affecting his nerves (as he intimated several times in media reports and interviews) as I have seen no similar reports connected to his other acting.

In 1961, Eric appeared in a British TV production called *A Call on Kuprin – Part 1*, though if there was a Part Two he clearly did not appear in it! The following year, a press report stated how he was taking an interest in local affairs, in his adopted home in Cornwall. He offered £100 as a reward encouraging people to discover the whereabouts of Fowey's early Victorian granite obelisk, which had stood on Albert Quay for nearly 100 years to mark the spot where Queen Victoria and the Prince Consort landed when they visited the town in 1846. Due to the increasing volume of traffic using the quay as a car park, the obelisk was demolished and sunk in the river off Penleath Point and subsequently located after Eric's offer. The money was won by a local man who discovered it on the bed of the harbour, though after much deliberation by the local council, it was decided that it should remain there.

On 22nd and 23rd June 1962, it was reported that "The Halifax-born actor, Eric Portman, of Duke of York Street, London, was injured last night last night, when a car, in which he was riding, turned over several times near Honiton, Devon, after swerving to avoid a collision. The driver, Mr George Bray, of Polperro, and another passenger, Mr Stuart Armfield, of the same address, were slightly injured. Mr Portman was admitted to hospital with severe shock and cuts.' The next day, he was said to be: "…very much rested and comfortable, at Marlpits Hospital, Honiton, Devon."

Eric Portman lived at Penpol. Here he is presenting a cheque to Dennis Rickman in 1965 for finding the broken obelisk in Fowey Harbour. Jack Vickers is behind him. William Hill is front left.

Eric hands over the 'reward' to the local man who located Fowey's lost obelisk! (Courtesy of the Cornish Guardian)

That year another film was released in which he appeared. Directed by John Huston, *Freud* was also released under the title *Freud: The Secret Passion*, and was notable for the fact that the original version of the script was written by the philosopher Jean-Paul Sartre.

The film stars Montgomery Clift in the title role and depicts five years (1885-1990) in the life of psychoanalyst Sigmund Freud, as he defied his colleagues' opinions, by using hypnosis to help his patients with their neuroses, and one patient in particular, Cecily Koertner, played by Susannah York. Eric is cast in a supporting role as Dr Theodore Meynert and the cast includes David McCallum, Allan Cuthbertson, David Kossoff, the voice of John Huston (who narrates the story) and a surprising name – Leonard Sachs – who will be better known to older readers as the presenter of former BBC programme *The Good Old Days*.

However, Eric later recounted how his appearance in the film *Freud*, never made it into the final edit. He said: 'I recommended a lady friend to see it, and at midnight she left a note in my letterbox saying I had been cut out. It was a bit of a shock!'

The next year, he appeared in two British crime films. One was *West 11*, directed by Michael Winner, starring Alfred Lynch, Kathleen Breck, Diana Dors, Finlay Currie, Francesca Annis, Patrick Wymark and also featured Harold Lang, who had appeared in several of Eric's previous films. In the second, he played Inspector Hofmeister in *The Man Who Finally Died*, a British thriller directed by Quentin Lawrence. It starred Stanley Baker, Peter Cushing, Mai Zetterling, Nigel Green, Niall MacGinnis, and Alfred Burke.

In April 1964, he returned to the stage, playing the title role in *The Claimant* by Robin Maugham, and when it was transferred to the Grand Theatre, Leeds, Eric was reported as occupying the same dressing room he had done 41 years earlier in 1923.

A journalist met him and described how the actor carefully fixed a sandy wig over his thinning hair and momentarily considered his reflection in the mirror. Then the actor squared his shoulders and swung round.

'There you are,' Eric told him. 'Not bad, is it, for 60? I've kept fit all my life. Plenty of walking, rest and the right food. I have never believed in burning the candle at both ends.'

It was further reported that his dressing room, one night, was packed with his friends and family, welcoming him home, and he spoke of his adopted county: "Cornwall has a sort of likeness to Yorkshire – but it is warmer there!"

His next film was *The Bedford Incident*, about the British-American Cold War, produced for Columbia Pictures and directed by James B. Harris. Starring Richard Widmark and Sidney Poitier, the cast also featured Martin Balsam, James MacArthur (who played Danno in the original TV series *Hawaii Five-O*) and with an early appearance for Donald Sutherland.

When the American Destroyer USS Bedford, detects a Soviet submarine in the GIUK gap near the Greenland coast, Captain Eric Finlander (Richard Widmark) mercilessly follows it, much to the alarm of others on the crew including civilian reporter Ben Munceford (Sidney Poitier) and Eric's character. When one of the Captain's men mistakes an order to fire a torpedo at the Russian submarine, the latter fires one back in retaliation, and so the ship is destroyed and the whole of the crew perish. In a twist on his character in *The 49th Parallel*, Eric plays Commodore Wolfgang Schrepke, an ex-World War Two U-Boat captain and one of the ill-fated crew. Eric commented that it was his favourite since playing Lieutenant Hurth, in that previous film.

Eric told journalist Michael Wale: 'I want to retire.' He had previously intimated about his retirement, but had recently felt that the time had arrived. However, there had been some dissenters. Firstly, he was offered the role in *The Bedford Incident*, and then came a letter from the owner of St Martin's Theatre, London, who said some flattering things and told him of a new play, *The Creeper*, which would be perfect for him.

So in July 1965, Eric returned to the stage to play Edward Kimberley in *The Creeper* at St Martin's Theatre, written by Pauline Macaulay and directed by Donald McWhinnie. The cast also featured Peter Blyth, Noel

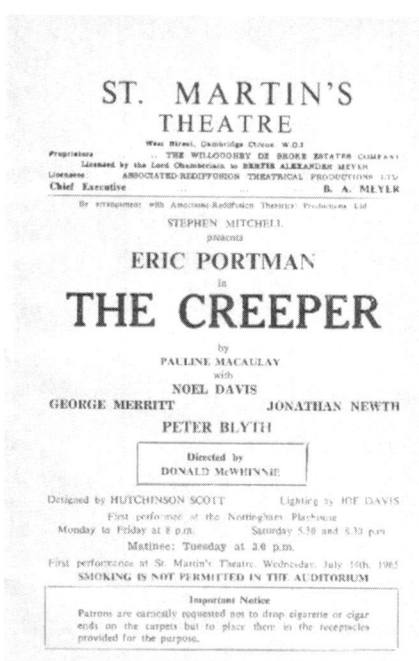

Advertising the play *The Creeper* (Courtesy of St Martin's Theatre)

'Eric Portman headlining the poster for *The Creeper* production (Courtesy of St Martin's Theatre)

Davis, Jonathan Newth and George Merritt.

A press report stated: 'Edward Kimberley…a millionaire, 57 years of age, lives in retirement in a vast mansion, Highgate, with an old family retainer, and a succession of young men – 'companions' whom he keeps up all night by playing the piano to – and gin rummy with – them…Eric Portman is the ideal cast for Edward Kimberley, the part is simply made for him.'

Which is a comment that could be taken either way. It could be construed as a compliment to the acting abilities of Eric – or perhaps a homophobic dig at the actor, for there had been questions raised at the time about his private life.

Regardless of this implication, though, one person who was pleased to renew his acquaintance was Irene Holloway, who would still meet him after each performance at the Garrick Theatre for a chat in his dressing room. She told me, '…we often used to walk from the stage door to the main road. I think that was possibly the last time I saw him.'

The playwright Pauline Macaulay told Tony Earnshaw: 'I met Eric Portman for the first time ever in Boston, America. I had gone over for a play he was in that my husband, Donald McWhinnie, was directing. I was writing *The Creeper* and I thought 'This is the actor that I want.' I'd always known him and liked him from movies but of course never dreamed I'd really get him. But I did. It was quite amazing because I was just a nobody. I stressed I wanted that actor and managements agreed with me, fortunately. (Eric) was highly nervous. He drank before he went on stage every night and sometimes he had one too many, but he very rarely went wrong. Eric was the only person for me. He had such a presence. And he did love the part. I can still hear his voice.'

One of Eric's co-stars in the play, Jonathan Newth, also spoke to Tony Earnshaw. The actor recalled: 'As a young actor approaching his first West End role, I was excited and apprehensive. It was 1965, the play was entitled *The Creeper* and the leading man was Eric Portman. My apprehension, beyond the actor's normal pre-rehearsal nerves, was fostered by the reputation of the star. In a business which thrives on in-house gossip, this reputation was not entirely flattering. While his talent was unquestioned, I was apprised of the 'facts' that he was (variously), waspish, aloof, given to bursts of temper, a heavy drinker and very secretive about his sexuality. Armed with this thumbnail sketch, supplied – needless to say mostly – by people who had never met or worked with EP, I entered the rehearsal room on the first day in a state of some anxiety. My experience of the man and the actor was entirely at odds with the compilation of characteristics I had been offered. To me, he could not have been kinder, more encouraging – or more tolerant; six months into the run I 'dried' (a bout of amnesia all actors dread when you have no idea what your next line is). After the performance, I went to apologise and to thank him for prompting me after what seemed like a five-minute hiatus. Eric simply dismissed it as one of those things that happen, an eminently sensible and reassuring reaction to any actor but particularly (to) a beginner whose confidence was severely shaken. Eric Portman was an immensely skilled actor from whom I, as a novice, learnt much about technique. His ability to suggest emotional and psychological depth and conflict with great economy was remarkable. I'm very glad that I had the opportunity to work with and get to know, a little, a complex and talented man.'

The journalist Michael Wale wrote how Eric appeared relaxed and calm, as the actor told him: 'Why do all these young people run around today worried about their age? And everyone is so concerned, especially American actors, after being a success. I'm sure they're all very young and very successful, but they don't really enjoy life, do they? They break down. They can't relax.'

In earlier years, he had told a reporter that acting was his whole life, but now said: 'Acting is still the most 'important' thing in my life. But the 'whole' life…? I don't know if I would call it that anymore. I have an interest in so many things. In fact, I'm interested in life altogether – fascinated by it. I don't believe in letting acting take up all my time and thoughts; some actors do, they join all kinds of theatrical organisations and are constantly busying themselves with theatrical affairs – I'm not like that. Some actors just can't bear to be away from it all.'

Eric spent much time at home in Penpol and evidently travelled to different parts of Cornwall. Roger Whear told me: 'In the mid-60s, my parents and I lived at Glynn House, near Bodmin Road Railway Station. On several occasions, my mother met Eric Portman at the station. She became quite enamoured with him and jokingly said to my father and I, that she would have run off with him! Apparently he had a wooden chalet near the station which he used.'

Eric's next film was *The Spy With A Cold Nose*, a British comedy directed by Daniel Petrie for Embassy Pictures, in 1966, and was written by Ray Galton and Alan Simpson, the famous writing partnership behind TV's *Steptoe and Son* and *Hancock's Half Hour*. The cast included Lawrence Harvey, Daliah Lavi, Lionel Jeffries, Eric Sykes, Denholm Elliott, Colin Blakely, June Whitfield, Robin Bailey, Michael Trubshawe and John Forbes-Robertson, with Eric playing 'The British Ambassador'.

It was probably the same year that he made a TV play called *The Crossfire*, broadcast on 3rd February 1967. Unfortunately, as with most of his TV work, it seems to have been lost to history, though I did receive an interesting snippet concerning the production.

Cazz Brill emailed me: 'Hi! I saw your letter in the *Daily Mirror*, and you brought back memories of when I was 19!! I'm now 64!! I was very young and training to be an assistant stage manager for Anglia Television, for a TV play called *The Crossfire*. Also in the show were Ian Hendry, Peter Wyngarde, Jeannette Sterke, Phillip Locke, Michael Coles, Roger Delgado, Wolfe Morris and Patrick Barr – and it was directed by John Jacobs. I remember having a drink in the bar with John Jacobs, Ian Hendry and Eric Portman. Eric wasn't happy about something in the script and was arguing with Ian Hendry, who he didn't have much time for.' (Caz thinks this only because of an age-gap). 'The argument was about some of the lines. Ian said it was one thing and Eric said it was something else. John Jacobs asked me to get the script, and I did so, but purposefully took a long time returning, because I knew Eric was wrong! I returned with the script, (but) by that time it was all resolved. Thank goodness!'

In 1967, Eric shared top billing with Dame Edith Evans in *The Whisperers*, a British drama directed and written by Bryan Forbes, and co-starring Nanette Newman, Gerald Sim, Ronald Fraser, Avis Bunnage and Kenneth Griffith. Dame Edith plays an impoverished elderly woman living in an apartment on her own, who leads a fantasy life as a heiress. She also thinks she can hear people plotting against her, whispering through the pipes in her room, though the people really plotting against her are her no-good son and husband. Despite the really grim plot with no happy ending, the movie won many plaudits and Dame Edith Evans won many awards for Best Actress in this film including a BAFTA and a Golden Globe.

Apart from being the director, Bryan Forbes had also written the script, saying that it included echoes of his parents' relationship in the film. He explained how he painted a portrait of two people, who could not communicate with each other. He recounted how his parents spent the last twenty years of their sixty-year marriage, communicating perfunctorily. He made Eric Portman say: 'People have to talk, have a conversation,' reflecting the poignancy of two people who share the same house and the same bed, yet have no common interests. Mr Forbes said he witnessed a slow deterioration between his parents and yet remained powerless to do anything about it.

Bryan Forbes must have been pleased with Eric's performance because in the next year he cast him opposite Michael Caine in another film he had written and directed entitled *Deadfall*.

Despite all the roles he had played in stage plays and movies, Eric later described his character as 'my best part since *The 49th Parallel*,' which may be partly due to the fact that his character, although married, is openly homosexual. As the law changed in 1967, decriminalising homosexuality, perhaps Eric felt it was time to play such a character.

The plot revolves around husband and wife, Fe and Richard Moreau (Giovanna Ralli and Eric Portman) who join forces with cat burglar Henry Clarke (Michael Caine). Again the cast featured Nanette Newman and also the celebrated comedy actor Leonard Rossiter. For the first time in his career, (with the possible exception of *The Creeper*) Eric played an openly gay man, Richard Moreau, who has a male lover, while having a wife, Fe Moraeu (Giovanna Ralli), who later turns out to be his daughter! The poster of the film included the tag-line: 'Michael Caine plunges into the world of the adulterous…the treacherous…and the perverse!'

Bryan Forbes, CBE, wrote to me: 'My view about Eric is that he was grossly overlooked when it came to handing out honours, because I considered him a superb actor, but always pursued by his own demons.'

Eric's last film as an actor was *Assignment To Kill* (1968), with a story about a private detective hired by an insurance company to investigate a shipping tycoon who is suspected of deliberately sinking his own ships in order to claim the insurance money.

Directed by Sheldon Reynolds, it starred Patrick O'Neal, Joan Hackett, John Gielgud, Herbert Lom, Oskar Homolka and Eric Portman played a character with no name; just a position – 'Notary'. He also appeared in the TV series *The Prisoner*, (Episode title: *Free For All*) starring Patrick McGoohan in the title role, which was broadcast on 20th October 1967. On the website www.theunmutual.co.uk which is dedicated to the TV series, Richard and Gaye Eastwood recounted their memories of working with Eric. Mrs Eastwood recalled: 'Eric Portman was a lovely fellow. He had a very nice lady with him who acted as a prompter, whom he relied on quite a lot.' Mr Eastwood added: 'I was on the balcony with him during the scene of the election campaign and they had to shoot this scene literally line by line. If they tried to do two lines together, he'd get through the first OK and halfway through the second, and then forget the rest of it. It went on like this over and over again.'

I received a letter from Jonathan McNicholl, who says 'Eric had been very ill after a stroke or heart-attack and afterwards had another one, I believe.' As far as I know, there were no press reports about Eric's condition, nor have I heard anything about it from the other people who contacted me, so perhaps details of this were not released to the press.

In 1968, Eric was offered a part in the play *Justice* by John Galsworthy, which opened at St Martins Theatre, London, and Mr McNicholl worked as Eric's dresser, helping him in the dressing room, both before and after each performance.

Advertising the play *Justice* (Courtesy of the Prince of Wales Theatre)

He told me: 'I worked as a dresser in London for twenty-five years from 1958 to 1983, only getting into that line of work quite by accident and so I did very well really. The play ran for six months and all the cast were male except Barbara Murray. She did not get on very well with Eric, I remember. Eric got on with men more easily than women. Unfortunately, he was known in the theatre as the actor who always made the Wardrobe Mistress cry. He could be demanding and always upset the women about something or other which did not satisfy him. Every actor has one or two little quirks which they are known for and I think that was the only 'bad' one that Eric had. Nothing actually nasty about it, just a habit he had. The cast included the TV actor Richard Briers and the play did a lot to help him in his career as he received some very good notices (reviews). I do not know much more about Eric (as some actors are quite private – and he was one of them), except that he was very friendly with Dirk Bogarde and did not like David Tomlinson at all, for some reason. I thought Eric's performance in *Justice* was one of his best ever. He was a nice man, very professional, and a wonderful actor with a beautiful voice. They do not make them like him nowadays.'

I wrote to various famous people who worked with Eric Portman, and the only person to reply, (apart from Bryan Forbes, CBE), was Richard Briers, also a CBE, best known for TV series' such as *The Good Life* and *Ever Decreasing Circles*, who sadly passed away in February 2013. Mr Briers phoned me up unexpectedly, quite out of the blue, and we had an interesting chat about his career, which included much theatre work and guest appearances in all sorts of TV programmes I had seen him in, ranging from *Lovejoy* to *Midsomer Murders*, and he also spoke of his time working with Eric Portman. As it happens, he had already spoken to the journalist and author Tony Earnshaw, about his work on *Justice*. As his comments to Tony read as a glowing tribute, I have used them as the Preface for the opening pages of this book.

Justice turned out to be the last theatre production Eric ever appeared in. When he began suffering dizzy spells at his flat, he consulted his doctors, who prescribed rest and retirement, which he had planned to do anyway, just evidently not so soon. He told a journalist: 'All three doctors told me to slow down because I was taxing my heart. I found on matinee days, that with only a quarter of an hour between shows, I was just completely exhausted. It really was getting too much for me. I suppose I could have carried on. But one hears such wretched things about one's friends popping off suddenly because they didn't heed their doctors. In a week, I had left my flat in St James's, and was installed in Cornwall in my lovely Wuthering Heights-type cottage.'

He bought an advertisement in *The Times* which read:

'Eric Portman would like to thank all those who have sent such understanding messages with regard to his enforced retirement from stage and TV. Luckily, he is still allowed to do radio work (if it should come his way). He remembers with gratitude the parts he has played in England and America and the immense fun he has always enjoyed with his friends both in and out of the dressing room.'

Eric lived quietly in Cornwall, away from the physical pressures of his work, but it was obvious to his friends that he missed the job which had been such a major driving force in his life for so long. Luckily, as Eric pointed out, radio acting was one of the concessions his doctors allowed him to do. He had been contracted to work on a radio programme, playing an ageing actor with a weak heart, presumably based on his own predicament, but he never completed it. Unfortunately, I can find no record of its title or whether the play was ever produced with a replacement actor.

In 1969, Terry Ladlow hired Eric to provide the narration for his short film *The Bronte Sisters*, which he made in association with the Bronte Society. He had originally asked two Yorkshire actors to make the recording: Eric Portman and Huddersfield-born actor James Mason – both of them with quite distinctive narrative tones. At the time, though, Mason was busy working on a film in Switzerland, but Eric agreed to do it.

Mr Ladlow told me: 'I contacted Eric through his agent, who gave me his address in Cornwall. It was two hours' work for the price of 50 guineas (approx £250) which was a very reasonable amount, considering he had to travel up to London from Cornwall.'

'However, Eric was unwell at the time, so we had to delay the recording for about a month until the actor said he was fit enough to travel. The session took around 90 minutes to complete, so I guess I was in his company for about two hours. He did it really well and gave the narration such an emotional feel and convinced the audience that he really loved the Bronte family and all that went with it.'

It was generally thought that Eric enjoyed his retirement (and in a previous interview he said he would be quite content on retirement) but he was a dedicated actor, particularly loving the theatre, and he obviously missed it. An unnamed friend, who had known him for 35 years, was later quoted as saying: 'He was putting a brave face on it.'

In addition to what little acting the doctors allowed him to do, Eric also continued to take an interest in local affairs in his adopted home in Cornwall. A newspaper reported how '…one of his most recent public appearances was at Bodmin Public Rooms in July when he officially opened Bodmin's Three Arts Festival.' The report described him as a well known figure in the village of Lerryn, adding that he had been a supporter of Lerryn Regatta, and that he also liked an occasional drink at the Ship Inn, at Lerryn.

Just three days after completing his narration on *The Bronte Sisters*, Eric visited the Ship Inn, and the licensee, Mr H. J. Phillips, later remarked: 'He called in at our place on Saturday for a short time and said he wasn't feeling very well.'

Returning home, Eric died peacefully in his sleep on 7th December 1969. Irene Holloway, fan and friend, lamented: 'Eric died – too early, I think

– for he still had so much more to give. But I shall always remember him with affection. Not only as a very fine actor but also as a very kind one.'

Knox Laing died five years later and is buried close to Eric in the churchyard at St Veep, near to the home that the actor so loved. Forever modest, never vain, Eric's memorial in the churchyard at St Veep reads:

Eric Portman
Actor
1901-1969

No waffle, no ego. Just that!

At the time of writing, (March 2013) there is a blue plaque outside Eric's home for much of his early life (number 20 Chester Road, Akroydon, Boothtown, Halifax) but it has not yet been replaced outside his actual birthplace (number 71). Local historian David Glover comments: 'Because of his success and the fact he was such a well-known figure, I wonder if there ought to be more than just a plaque in his memory. Perhaps a more substantial memory would be fitting.'

On 7th January 1970, exactly one month after Eric's death, Miss Joyce Broadfield, of Widnes, wrote to the *Halifax Courier*:

'I have been a keen fan of Eric Portman since I was fifteen when, during the dark days of the war, he enriched our lives with his magnificent film performances. In 1948, I had the pleasure of seeing him on the stage at the Opera House, Manchester, in *The Browning Version*. Again in Manchester, I had the pleasure of shaking hands with him in the foyer of a cinema after he had made a personal appearance. There have been many great actors –

but very few men like Eric Portman. He remained completely unaffected by his fame. In a profession in which there is so much gossip and scandal, his personal life was above reproach. The gossip writers were unable to include his name in their columns throughout more than forty years in his profession. I wrote two fan letters to him in the 1940s and received replies to both. Last summer, after reading of his illness, I wrote again. I was surprised and delighted to receive a two-page handwritten letter in reply. In it, he mentioned the North Country and I have reason to believe that, although he delighted in his Cornish surroundings, he still had great affection for Yorkshire.'

'It is sad to think that anyone under the age of 40 must be too young to remember his films. In 20 or 30 years there will be very few people who remember him at all. I would like to suggest, therefore, that consideration be given to perpetuating his name in his hometown of Halifax or nearby. The Leeds Playhouse which is now being built could be called The Eric Portman Theatre. Failing that, perhaps there is some building in Halifax that will suffice.' (Courtesy of Halifax Courier Ltd)

As it happens, some building in Halifax *did* suffice, just over ten years later. A public house in the town was refurbished and reopened and they ran a competition in the *Halifax Courier*, for someone to suggest a new name for it. The winning entry was for The Portman and Pickles, named after Eric and his old friend Wilfred Pickles – the two local lads made good. The name continued until 2012, when the pub was refurbished yet again and renamed The Jubilee, although, at the time of writing, there are still framed press cuttings about Eric and Wilfred on the walls of the pub and two or three other features adorned with the 'P&P' logo.

Many years earlier, R. Quilter Vincent, who seems to have interviewed

Eric more than any other journalist, gave an example of the actor's generosity, which may provide a fitting tribute:

'He is a cheerful person, always jovial, amusing and exceedingly generous. One hesitates before ascribing the normal kind of generosity, for he is generous to a degree not often found among people of prominence. I remember with pleasure the occasion at a dance held by some film studio workers, when he was approached by the organiser for his autograph to raffle for the Studio Workers' Benevolent Fund. Portman said at once: 'But wouldn't it be better for your benevolent fund if you had my autograph on a cheque?' he asked with a smile, and thereupon wrote out a cheque for a sum which made the organiser gasp.'

'If warm-heartedness, sincerity and a genuine and absorbing interest in his work count for anything, then Eric is lucky, for he has all three. I count him among my most valuable friends. His lack of 'star-complex', his genuine friendliness and co-operation with his fellow actors and studio workers (who adore him, call him 'Eric', and say that he is one of the most unaffected of all our stars) are prominent features of his attitude to his work. He is talented and likeable, surely an agreeable combination?'

I will leave the last words about Eric to C. E. D. Bottomley who wrote a letter to the *Halifax Courier*, shortly after the actor's death:

'It is pleasing that Eric Portman achieved such fame. He was a splendid type of man.'
(Courtesy of the Halifax Courier Ltd)

APPENDIX

FILMS/RADIO/TV

Eric Portman's known films, radio plays, documentaries and TV productions (such as one-off plays, made-for-TV films and episodes of TV series').

The Girl from Maxim's (1933)
Leslie Henson, Frances Day, George Grossmith Jr, Lady Tree, Stanley Holloway, Gertrude Musgrove, Evan Thomas, Desmond Jeans, Hugh Dempster, **Eric Portman (uncredited)**.
Director: Alexander Korda.

Chu Chin Chow (1934)
George Robey, Fritz Kortner, Anna May Wong, Pearl Argyle, Sydney Fairbrother, Dennis Hoey, Lawrence Hanray, Frank Cochrane, Gibb McLaughlin,, Francis L. Sullivan, Kiyoshi Takase, Nils Asther, Adrienne Ames, John Stuart, Walter Rilla, Patric Knowles, Annie Esmond, Arthur Hardy, Clifford Heatherley, **Eric Portman**, Warren Jenkins.
Director: Karl Grune

Maria Marten, or The Murder in the Red Barn (1935)
Tod Slaughter, Sophie Stewart, D.J. Williams, **Eric Portman**, Clare Greet, Gerard Tyrell, Ann Trevor, Stella Rho, Dennis Hoey, Quentin McPhearson, Antonia Brough, Noel Dainton.
Director: Milton Rosmer

Hyde Park Corner (1935)
Gordon Harker, Binnie Hale, **Eric Portman**, Gibb McLaughlin, Harry Tate, Robert Holmes, Eileen Peel, Donald Wolfit.
Director: Sinclair Hill

Old Roses (1935)
Horace Hodges, Nancy Burne, Bruce Lester, Charles Mortimer, Felix Aylmer, Wilfred Walter, Esme Church, George Hayes, **Eric Portman**, Trevor Jones.
Director: Bernard Mainwaring.

Abdul the Damned (1935)
Fritz Kortner, Adrienne Ames, Nils Asther, John Stuart, Esme Percy, Walter Rilla, Patric Knowles, **Eric Portman**.
Director: Karl Grune

Hearts of Humanity (1936) (Alternative titles: *Crypt* and *Abide with Me*)
Bransby Williams, Wilfred Walter, Cathleen Nesbitt, Pamela Randall, **Eric Portman**, Hay Petrie, J. Fisher White, Fred Duprez.
Director: John Baxter

The Cardinal (1936)
Matheson Lang, **Eric Portman**, Robert Atkins, O. B. Clarence, Douglas Jefferies, F. B. J. Sharp, Wilfred Fletcher, A. Bromley Davenport, Rayner Barton, Edgar K. Bruce, David Horne, June Duprez, Henrietta Watson, Dora Barton.
Director: Sinclair Hill

The Crimes of Stephen Hawke (1936)
Tod Slaughter, Marjorie Taylor, D. J. Williams, **Eric Portman**, Graham Soutten.
Director: George King

Moonlight Sonata (1937)
Ignace Paderewski, **Eric Portman**, Marie Tempest, Charles Farrell, Barbara Greene, Binkie Stuart.
Director: Lothar Mendes

The Prince and the Pauper (1937)
Errol Flynn, Billy Mauch, Bobby Mauch, Claude Rains, Barton MacLane, Henry Stephenson, Alan Hale, Sr., Montagu Love, Halliwell Hobbes, Rupert Warwick, **Eric Portman**.
Director: William Keighley

The Singing Marine (1937)
Dick Powell, Doris Weston, Jane Darwell, Hugh Herbert, Lee Dixon, Dick Wesson, Allen Jenkins, Jane Wyman, Larry Adler, **Eric Portman**.
Director: Ray Enright

The Constant Nymph – TV movie (1938)
Eric Portman (also featured Ronald Shiner)

A Hundred Years Old – TV movie (1938)
Eric Portman (Trino)

The Rivals – TV movie (1938)
Eric Portman (Captain Absolute)

The Gamblers – TV movie (1939)
Eric Portman (Iharyof)

She Stoops To Conquer – TV movie (1939)
Eric Portman (Young Marlow)

A Night at the Hardcastles – TV movie (1939)
Eric Portman (also featured the actress Celia Johnson)

The Pelican – TV movie (1939)
Eric Portman (Charles Cheriton)

The 49th Parallel (1941)
Laurence Olivier, Leslie Howard, Raymond Massey, Anton Walbrook, **Eric Portman**, Glynis Johns, Finlay Currie, Niall MacGinnis.
Director: Michael Powell

One of Our Aircraft is Missing (1942)
Godfrey Tearle, **Eric Portman**, Hugh Williams, Bernard Miles, Hugh Burden, Emrys Jones, Googie Withers, Pamela Brown, Joyce Redman, Googie Withers, Hay Petrie, Selma Van Dias, Arnold Marle, Robert Helpmann, Peter Ustinov, Alec Clunes.
Director: Michael Powell and Emeric Pressburger

Uncensored (1942)
Eric Portman, Phyllis Calvert, Griffith Jones, Raymond Lovell, Peter Glenville, Irene Handel, Felix Aylmer, Eliot Makeham, John Slater, Aubrey Mallalieu, Frederick Culley, Carl Jaffe, Walter Hudd, J. H. Roberts, Peter Godfrey.
Director: Anthony Asquith.

Squadron Leader X (1942)
Eric Portman, Ann Dvorak, Walter Fitzgerald, Martin Miller, Beatrice Varley, Henry Oscar, Barry Jones, Charles Victor, Marjorie Rhodes, David Peel, Aubrey Mallalieu, Carl Jaffe. Director: Lance Comfort

We Dive at Dawn (1943)
John Mills, **Eric Portman**, Niall MacGinnis, Louis Bradfield, Ronald Millar, Jack watling, Reginald Purdell, Caven Watson, Leslie Weston, Norman

Williams, Lionel Grose, David Peel, Philip Godfrey, Robb Wilton, Walter Gotell.
Director: Anthony Asquith

Escape To Danger (1943)
Eric Portman, Ann Dvorak, Karel Stepanek, Ronald Ward, Ronald Adam, Felix Aylmer, Brefniu O'Rorke, A.E. Matthews, Ivor Barnard, David Peel, Charles Victor, George Merritt, Marjorie Rhodes, John Ruddock, Frederick Cooper.
Directors: Lance Comfort and Victor Hanbury

Millions Like Us (1943)
Anne Crawford, Gordon Jackson, Patricia Roc, Basil Radford, Naunton Wayne, Moore Marriott, **Eric Portman**, Joy Shelton, John Boxer, Valentine Dunn, Megs Jenkins, Terry Randall, Amy Veness, Beatrice Varley, Bertha Willmott.
Directors: Sidney Gilliat and Frank Launder

A Canterbury Tale (1944)
Eric Portman, Sheila Sim, Dennis Price, Sgt John Sweet, Esmond Knight, Charles Hawtrey, Hay Petrie, George Merritt, Edward Rigby, Freda Jackson, Betty Jardine, Eliot Makeham, Harvey Golden, Leonard Smith, James Tamsitt.
Directors: Michael Powell and Emeric Pressburger

Great Day (1945)
Eric Portman, Flora Robson, Sheila Sim, Isabel Jeans, Walter Fitzgerald, Philip Friend, Marjorie Rhodes, Maire O'Neill, John Laurie, Kathleen Harrison, Leslie Dwyer, Margaret Withers, Beatrice Varley, Irene Handel, Patricia Hayes.
Director: Lance Comfort

The Air Plan (1945)
Royal Air Force documentary
Eric Portman (narrator)

Wanted for Murder (1946) (alternative title: *A Voice in the Night*)
Eric Portman, Dulcie Gray, Derek Farr, Roland Culver, Stanley Holloway, Barbara Everest, Bonar Colleano, Jenny Laird, Kathleen Harrison, Bill Shine, Viola Lyel, John Salew, John Ruddock, Edna Wood, George Carney.
Director: Lawrence Huntington

Men of Two Worlds (1946)
Robert Adams, **Eric Portman**, Orlando Martins, Phyllis Calvert, Arnold Marle, Cathleen Nesbitt.
Director: Thorold Dickinson

Dear Murderer (1947)
Eric Portman, Greta Gynt, Dennis Price, Maxwell Reed, Jack Warner, Hazel Court, Jane Hylton, Andrew Crawford.
Director: Arthur Crabtree

The Mark of Cain (1947)
Sally Gray, **Eric Portman**, Patrick Holt, Dermot Walsh, Dennis O'Dea, Edward Lexy, Miles Malleson.
Director: Brian Desmond

Corridor of Mirrors (1948)
Eric Portman, Edana Romney, Barbara Mullen, Hugh Sinclair, Bruce Belfrage, Alan Wheatley, Joan Maude, Leslie Weston, Christopher Lee, Hugh Latimer, John Penrose, Lois Maxwell, Mavis Villiers.
Director: Terence Young

Daybreak (1948)
Eric Portman, Ann Todd, Maxwell Reed, Bill Owen, Edward Rigby, Jane Hylton, Eliot Makeham, Margaret Withers, John Turnbull, Maurice Denham, Milton Rosmer.
Director: Compton Bennett

The Blind Goddess (1948)
Eric Portman, Anne Crawford, Hugh Williams, Michael Denison, Claire Bloom, Elspet Gray, Nora Swinburne, Martin Benson, Raymond Lovell, Clive Morton, Maurice Denham, Cecil Bevan, Frank Cellier.
Director: Harold French

The Spider and The Fly (1949)
Eric Portman, Guy Rolfe, Nadia Gray, George Cole, John Carol, Harold Lang, Edward Chapman, Maurice Denham, John Salew, May Hallatt, James Hayter, Arthur Lowe.
Director: Robert Hamer

Cairo Road (1950)
Eric Portman, Laurence Harvey, Maria Mauban, Harold Lang, Gregoire Aslan, Karel Stepanek, John Bailey, Martin Boddey, John Gregson, Marne Maitland, John Harvey, Abraham Sofaer, Peter Jones.
Director: David MacDonald

The Magic Box (1951)
Robert Donat, Margaret Johnston, Maria Schell, David Oake, Janette Scott, John Howard Davies, Robert Beatty, Richard Attenborough, Basil Sydney, Bernard Miles, **Eric Portman**, Mary Ellis, Muir Mathieson, Joyce Grenfell, Dennis Price, Margaret Rutherford, Mervyn Johns, Glynis Johns, Frederick Valk.
Cameos:
Barry Jones, Bessie Love, Cecil Parker, David Tomlinson, Emlyn Williams,

Ernest Thesiger, Kay Walsh, Laurence Olivier, Jack Hulbert, Leo Genn, Marius Goring, Michael Denison, Michael Hordern, Miles Malleson, Peter Ustinov, Sheila Sim, Sid James, Stanley Holloway, Thora Hird, William Hartnell, Ronald Shiner, Googie Withers, A. E. Matthews, John McCallum, Patric Holt, Robertson Hare, Richard Murdoch, Sybil Thorndike, Henry Edwards.
Director: John Boulting

Painter and Poet No. 2 (part three: *Check to Song*)
(**narrator: Eric Portman**) This was a documentary in three parts for the British Film Institute, of which Eric narrated the third segment. The first two were narrated by Michael Redgrave and Stanley Holloway.

His Excellency (1952)
Eric Portman, Cecil Parker, Helen Cherry, Susan Stephen, Edward Chapman, Clive Morton, Alec mango, Geoffrey Keen, John Salew, Robin Bailey, Eric Pohlmann.
Director: Robert Hamer

South of Algiers (1953)
Van Heflin, Wanda Hendrix, **Eric Portman**, Charles Goldner, Jacques B. Brunius, Jacques Francois, Aubrey Mather, Simone Silva, Marne Maitland, George Pastell, Alec Mango.
Director: Jack Lee.

Jeannie (1954) – BBC Sunday-Night Theatre (TV series)
Eric Portman (Stanley Smith)

The Colditz Story (1955)
John Mills, **Eric Portman**, Christopher Rhodes, Lionel Jeffries, Bryan Forbes, Guido Lorraine, Anton Diffring, Richard Wattis, Ian Carmichael, Frederick

Valk, Denis Shaw, Theodore Bikel, Keith Pyott, Eugene Deckers, Anthony Faramus, Peter Swanwick.
Director: Guy Hamilton

The Deep Blue Sea (1955)
Vivien Leigh, Kenneth More, **Eric Portman**, Emlyn Williams, Moira Lister, Alec McCowan, Dandy Nichols, Jimmy Hanley, Miriam Karlin, Heather Thatcher, Bill Shine, Brian Oulton, Gibb McLaughlin, Arthur Hill, Sidney James.
Director: Anatole Litvak

Mister Betts Runs Away (1955) – Theatre Royal (TV series)
Eric Portman (Mr Betts)

The Last Reunion (1955) *ITV Television Playhouse* (TV series)
Eric Portman (Simmie)

The Case of Private Hamp (1955) – Radio play for the BBC Home Service.

The Case of Dr Crippen (1956) – Theatre Royal – (TV series)
Eric Portman (Dr Hawley Harvey Crippen)

Child in the House (1956)
Phyllis Calvert, **Eric Portman**, Stanley Baker, Mandy Miller, Dora Bryan, Joan Hickson, Victor Maddern, Percy Herbert, Joan Benham, Martin Miller, Christopher Toyne, Molly Urquhart, Bruce Beeby, Peter Burton, Maggie Smith, Alfie Bass.
Director: Cy Endfield

A Double Life (1957) – *The Alocoa Hour* – TV series
Eric Portman (Anthony John / Othello)

203

The Good Companions (1957)
Eric Portman, Celia Johnson, Hugh Griffith, Janette Scott, John Fraser, Joyce Grenfell, Bobby Howes, Rachel Roberts, John Salew, Mona Washbourne, Paddy Stone.
Director: J. Lee Thompson.

A Tale of Two Cities (1958) – *The DuPont Show of the Month*, TV series
Eric Portman (Dr Manette)

Oliver Twist (1959) – *The DuPont Show of the Month*, TV series
Eric Portman (Fagin)

Victory (1960) – *The Art Carney TV Show*, (TV series)
Eric Portman (also featured the actor Richard Harris)

The Hero (1960) – *Alfred Hitchcock Presents...* (TV series)
Eric Portman (Sir Richard Musgrave)

Twentieth Century Theatre – The Elder Statesman (1960) *BBC Sunday Night Play* (TV series)
Eric Portman (Lord Claverton)

Naked City (1960) (TV series) Episode: *The Pedigree Sheet*
Eric Portman (Jayson Condon)

Duet For Two Hands (1960) – *Play of the Week* (TV series)
Eric Portman (Dr Edward Sarclet)

The Terrible Clockman (1961) – *Shirley Temple's Storybook* (TV series)
Eric Portman (Van Der Graf)

A Call on Kuprin – Part One (1961) TV play.
Eric Portman

The Naked Edge (1961)
Gary Cooper, Deborah Kerr, **Eric Portman**, Diane Cilento, Hermione Gingold, Peter Cushing, Michael Wilding, Ronald Howard, Ray McAnally, Sandor Eles, Wilfred Lawson, Helen Cherry, Joyce Carey, Diane Clare, Frederick Leister.
Director: Michael Anderson

The Last Reunion (1961) *ITV Television Playhouse* (TV series)
Eric Portman

Freud (1962) also released as *Freud: The Secret Passion*
* **Eric's performance was cut from the final edit.**
Montgomery Clift, Susannah York, Larry Parks, Susan Kohmer, Eileen Herlie, Fernand Ledoux, David McCallum, Rosalie Crutchley, David Kossoff, Joseph Furst, Alexander Mango, Leonard Sachs, John Huston, Vistor Beaumont, Allan Cuthbertson, Maria Perschy, Moira Redmond
Director: John Huston

Love Story (TV series). Episode – *The Habit of Loving*
Eric Portman (also featured the actress Lana Young, and the episode was written by Doris Lessing)

West 11 (1963)
Alfred Lynch, Kathleen Breck, **Eric Portman**, Diana Dors, Kathleen Harrison, Finlay Currie, Freda Jackson, peter Reynolds, Harold Lang, Marie Ney, Sean Kelly, Patrick Wymark, Ken Colyer, Alan McClelland, Franscesca Annis.
Director: Michael Winner

The Man Who Finally Died (1963)
Stanley Baker, Peter Cushing, Mai Zetterling, **Eric Portman**, Nigel Green, Georgina Ward, Niall MacGinnis, Barbara Everest, Harold Scott, Alfred Burke, James Ottaway, Mela White, Maya Sorell.
Director: Quentin Lawrence

The Bedford Incident (1965)
Richard Widmark, Sidney Poitier, **Eric Portman**, James McArthur, Martin Balsam, Wally Cox, Ed Bishop, Donald Sutherland.
Director: James B. Harris

The Spy With A Cold Nose (1966)
Laurence Harvey, Daliah Lavi, Lionel Jeffries, Eric Sykes, **Eric Portman**, Denholm Elliott, Colin Blakely, June Whitfield, Robert Flemyng, Bernard Archard, Robin Bailey, Genevieve, Nai Bonet, Paul Ford, Michael Trubshawe, Bruce Carstairs, Glen Mason, Norma Foster, Gillian Lewis, Wanda Ventham, Amy Dalby, Tricia De Dulin, Virginia Lyon, Julian Orchard, John Forbes-Robertson, Arnold Diamond.
Director: Daniel Petrie

The Crossfire (1967) – *ITV Play of the Week* (TV series)
Eric Portman (Dr David Sorel)

The Whisperers (1967)
Edith Evans, **Eric Portman**, Nanette Newman, Harry Baird, Jack Austin, Gerald Sim, Lionel Gamlin, Glen Farmer, Olivier MacGreevy, Ronald Fraser, Kenneth Griffith, Avis Bunnage, John Orchard, Peter Thompson, Sarah Forbes, Penny Spencer, Rajesh Kera.
Director: Bryan Forbes

The Prisoner (1967) TV Series Episode: *Free For All*
Eric Portman (Number Two)

Deadfall (1968)
Michael Caine, Giovanna Ralli, **Eric Portman**, David Buck, Leonard Rossiter, Geraldine Sherman, Carlos Pierre, Vladek Sheybal, Renata Tarrago, Nanette Newman.
Director: Bryan Forbes

Assignment To Kill (1968)
Patrick O'Neal, Joan Hackett, John Gielgud, Herbert Lom, Oscar Homolka, **Eric Portman**.
Director: Sheldon Reynolds

Strange Report (1969) TV series. Episode: *Skeleton: Let Sleeping Heroes Lie*
Eric Portman (Elleston)

The Bronte Sisters (1969)
Director: Terry Ladlow
Eric Portman (narrator)

STAGE PLAYS

1924,
Victorian Theatre, Sunderland.
Character not known; *Richard II*

Sept 1924,
Savoy Theatre, London.
Antipholus of Syracruse in *The Comedy of Errors*
and Mowbray in *Richard II*

1925,
Strand,
Worthing in *White Cargo*

1926-1927, toured in a repertory of modern plays:
Rudolf Steiner Hall:
Orestes in *Electra*

Old Vic,
Horatio in *Hamlet*

Joined the Old Vic Theatre Company at the Lyric, Hammersmith.
Sept 1927 - Jan 1928
Lucentio in *The Taming of the Shrew*
Bassanio the Dauphin in *Henry V*
Claudio in *Much Ado About Nothing*

1928,
The Old Vic,
Romeo in *Romeo and Juliet*
Charles Surface in *A School for Scandal*
Edmund in *King Lear*
Arcite in *The Two Noble Kinsmen*
Laertes in *Hamlet*
Strength in *Everyman*

October to November 1928,
Arts Theatre,
Erhard Borkman in *John Gabriel Borkman*
Kaleve in Caravan.

January 1929,
Queens Theatre,
Berthold in *The Mock Emperor*

March 1929,
Wyndham's Theatre,
Stephen Undershaft in *Major Barbara*

July 1929,
Arts Theatre,
Robert in *The Hell Within*

August 1929,
Q Theatre,
Edward Adishan in *Portrait of a Lady*

November 1929,
Vaudeville Theatre,
Tony in *The Roof*

February 1930,
Court Theatre,
Laertes in *Hamlet*

March 1930,
Gate Theatre,
Le Vicomte in *The Lion Tamer*

March 1930,
Court Theatre,
Joseph Percival in *Misalliance*

April 1930,
Lyric Hammersmith
Crowley Tukes in *Out of the Blue*
Young Marlow in *She Stoops to Conquer*

June 1930,
Royalty Theatre,
Aimwell in *The Beaux Strategem*

October 1930,
Embassy Theatre
Lelio in *The Liar*

Feb 1931,
Gate Theatre,
Eben in *Desire Under The Elms*

Sept 1931,
Lyric Hammersmith
Bellmour in *The Old Bachelor*

Nov 1931,
Duchess Theatre,
Ragnar Brovik in *The Master Builder*

Feb 1932,
Gate Theatre,
Paul in '*Which…?*'

October 1932,
Embassy Theatre,
George D'Alroy in *Caste*

May 1933,
Captain Absolute in *The Rivals*
George von Hartwig in *Midsummer Fires*

May 1933,
Princes Theatre,
Count Orloff in *Diplomacy*

Sept 1933,
Wyndham's Theatre,
Ernest Turner in *Sheppey*

November 1933,
Apollo Theatre,
Thomas Lawrence in *Mrs Siddons*

December 1933,
Playhouse,
Hubert Capes in *The World of Light*

1934,
New Theatre,
Robert De Vere in *Richard of Bordeaux*

Sept 1934,
Embassy Theatre,
Murat in *Napoleon*

November 1934,
Piccadilly for Repertory Players,
Carlo Monreale in *Our Mutual Father*

November 1934,
Shaftesbury,
Dante Aligheri in *For Ever*

March to May 1935,
Daly's Theatre,
Adrian Adair in *Chase The Ace*

July 1935,
Criterion Theatre,
Edward Tramley in *This Desirable Residence*

January 1936,
Arts Theatre,
Lord Byron in *Bitter Harvest*

May 1936,
St Martin's,
same role and play

June 1937,
New Theatre,
Victor Brun in *The New Romancer*

July 1937,
Open Air Theatre,
Brutus in *Julius Caesar*

November 1937,
Broadhurst Theatre in New York
Rodolph Boulanger in *Madame Bovary*

April 1938,
Gate Theatre, London,
Crown Prince Rudolph in *The Masque of Kings*

August 1938,
The Comedy Theatre,
Richard Dahl in *Give Me Yesterday*

October 1938,
Guild Theatre in New York
Oliver Farrant in *I Have Been Here Before*

May 1939,
Wyndham's Theatre, London,
Blaise Lebel in *The Intruder*

November 1939,
Embassy Theatre,
Mark Anthony in *Julius Caesar* (play performed in modern dress)

December 1939,
His Majesty's Theatre,
same role/play

Feb 1940,
Torch Theatre, London
Stanley Smith in *Jeannie*

April 1940,
Wyndham's,
same play and same role

Feb 1943
toured through the UK
Harry Quincey in *Uncle Harry*

May 1944,
Duke of York's Theatre
Stephen Marlowe in *Zero Hour*

Sept 1948,
Phoenix Theatre,
Andrew Crocker-Harris in *The Browning Version* and Arthur Gosport in *Harlequinade*, with the umbrella title: *Playbill*

May 1950,
Princes' Theatre
The Governor in *His Excellency*.

Novermber 1951,
Adelphi Theatre,
The Marshall in *The Moment of Truth*

Sept 1952,
Opera House, Manchester
Sir Robert Briston in *The Guilty Party*

April 1953,
Wyndhams London
Father James Brown in *The Living Room*

February 1954,
Wyndhams, London
Mark Heath in *Shadow of the Vine*

Sept 1954,
St James's and UK tour
Mr Martin in *Table by the Window* and Major Pollock in *Table Number Seven*; both played under the umbrella title *Separate Tables*

October 1956-January 1958,
Played the same parts at the Music Box Theatre, Broadway, New York, and also on tour in America.

May 1958,
Belasco Theatre, New York,
Mr Rochester in *Jane Eyre*

October 1958,
Helen Hayes Theatre, New York,
Cornelius Melody in *A Touch of the Poet*

October 1959,
Lyceum, New York
Jim Cherry in *Flowering Cherry*

January 1962,
Ambassador Theatre, New York
Mr Fielding in *A Passage to India*

April 1964,
The Comedy Theatre, London.
Title role in The *Claimant*

July 1965,
St Martin's Theatre, London.
Edward Kimberley in *The Creeper*

1968
St Martin's Theatre, London.
Justice

Desert Island Discs
Eric Portman's musical choices were:

1. Le Fiacre (Jean Sablon)
2. Lehar – The Merry Widow Waltz (Marek Weber and his Orchestra)
3. Because (Eva Turner)
4. Cancoes de Criances (Peter Kreuder on piano)
5. Mendelssohn's Midsummer Nights' Dream (intermezzo) – (Amsterdam Concert getouw/Van Beinum)
6. Cool Water (Nellie Lutcher)
7. Maladie d'amour (Henri Salvador)
8. A Voice in the Night – from the film *Wanted For Murder* (Eric Harrison on piano, and Queen's Hall Light Orchestra)

BIBLIOGRAPHY/SOURCES

BOOKS

Aldgate Anthony and Jeffrey Richards, *Britain Can Take It: The British Cinema in the Second World War* (Basil Blackwell, 1984; Edinburgh University Press, 1994)

Blakeston, O., (editor) *Working for the Films* (1947) (London: Focal Press); includes Eric Portman's essay *The Film Actor*

Darlow, Michael, *Terence Rattigan: The Man and His Work* (Quartet Books, 2000)

Duff, Charles, *The Lost Summer: The Heyday of the West End Theatre* (Nick Hern Books, 1995)

Forbes, Bryan, *A Divided Life* (William Heinemann, 1993; Mandarin Books, 1993)

Lee, Stephanie, *British Film Stars at Home* (Findan, 1948)

Pickles, Wilfred, *Between You and Me* (Werner Laurie, 1949)

NEWSPAPERS AND MAGAZINES

Halifax Courier, Yorkshire Post, Rotherham Advertiser, Yorkshire Observer, Cornish Guardian, Daily Sketch, Daily Herald, Radio Times, TV Times, Picturegoer, The Queen, Film World, Film Quarterly, Film Illustrated Monthly, ABC Film Review, Yorkshire Illustrated.

ACKNOWLEDGEMENTS

All known copyright owners have been contacted for necessary permissions, though there are several sources which remain unidentified. If anyone can help with identifying owners, please could you contact me through my website address above?

A big thank you to the Editor, staff and owners of Halifax Courier Ltd, for allowing me into their offices to find information about Eric Portman and for the Editor's permission to reproduce much copyright material – both text and photographs – from the newspaper. Particular thanks to the editor John Kenealy, and journalists Kathryn Allan and David Hanson. Their website is: www.halifaxcourier.co.uk.

Also to the following for permission to reproduce copyright text, photographs and press clippings: Peter Charlton, Editor of the *Yorkshire Post* and also the owners of Yorkshire Post Newspapers Ltd; Andrew Mosley, Editor of the *Rotherham Advertiser*; Zena O'Rourke, Editor of the *Cornish Guardian*; David Hodges of the *Radio Times*; Thanks to the unknown owners of *The Herald* and *The Daily Sketch*; Paula Straw and all at Halifax Light Opera Society for permission to reproduce the Eric Portman photograph from their theatre programme; to St Martin's Theatre, The Adelphi Theatre and the Prince of Wales' Theatre, all in London, for permission to reproduce copyright material from their theatre programmes. Also to Jeanne O'Rourke of the Halifax Thespians for lending me a scrapbook full of photographs and press cuttings about Eric Portman, together with Marion Reynolds and Brenda Chapel of the Halifax Thespians.

A big thank you to Professor Andrew Spicer of the University of West England, and author of the article 'The Mark of Cain: Eric Portman and Stardom', which is available to read online. Additional thanks to Andrew for sending me lots of articles about Eric Portman's career, and for writing a Foreword for this book; Tony Earnshaw, journalist, author and partner of www.reelsolutions.co.uk for allowing me to quote from the extensive research he did for his presentation 'A Tribute to Eric Portman' which was held in Halifax, in July 2012. Deryck Botterill of St Bartholomew's Church and Elizabeth St John of St Veep Church, both in Cornwall, for gaining photographs of Eric and Knox's graves in the grounds of St Veep Parish Church; Lynn Goold of Fowey Information for sending me a copy of Eric's What Fowey Means To Me article; Library staff at The National Film Institute, National Media Museum and National Portrait Gallery; Thanks to owners of countless websites (too many to mention) including Screen Online, Rotten Tomatoes, and major help from the brilliant Wikipedia. Michael Darlow and Barbara Longford of the Terence Rattigan Society; Staff of Calderdale Reference Library for much help including access to archives; The staff of Halifax Register Office for help and advice with research; Gwen Rudman for sending me lots of articles and other information about Eric Portman; Stephen Gee for help with archive photographs of Halifax; Paul Weatherhogg of the Lerryn Historical Society; David Glover, Halifax historian, of the Halifax Civic Trust for much help including his discovery of Eric's true birthday and place of birth; Dan Sudron and John Patchett of the West Yorkshire Archive Service; Trish Hayes of BBC Written Archives Centre, Berkshire; Lynn Humphries of Sheffield Archives; Steve Crook and his fascinating website www.powell-pressburger.org dedicated to the films of Michael Powell and Emeric Pressburger; Rick Davy for allowing me to reproduce copyright material from his website www.theunmutual.co.uk dedicated to the TV series The Prisoner; Kim Cooper of the Cornish Studies Library/Cornwall Centre; Kevin Hopkinson of Yorkshire's nostalgic magazine Down Your Way; Mike Ferguson for sending me his photo of Knox Laing; The Editors and staff of the Daily Mirror; The Stage; Choice; The Cornishman; Cornish Guardian, The Dalesman; Down Your Way; Evergreen; Mature Times; Western Daily Press; Express and Star and many, many other publications which carried details of my media appeal – unfortunately far too many to list here. Also thanks to the former editors, publishers and copyright owners of various newspapers and movie magazines for all their valuable work amassing information about Eric Portman, and to the journalists who interviewed him including Leonard Wallace, Michael Wale, Edith Nepean, Gordon Musgrove, John Y. Stapelton and R. Quilter Vincent and to the critics who reviewed his plays, TV and films.

Also many thanks to the following people who replied to my media appeal via letter or email: Victor Azzopardi; Marcia Bell; Cazz Brill; Sue Brown; A. M. Burnell; Betty Breheny; Richard Briers, CBE; Christine Broom (nee Whetter); Terry Christie; Vanessa Clark (nee Portman); Stuart Connell; J. W. Connolly; Kim Cooper; Daphne Crawshaw; Tim Dixon; Florence Dunn; Patricia Duggan (nee Portman); Patricia M. Emmanuel; John and Barbara Ferguson; Mike Ferguson; Bryan Forbes, CBE; Mr F. Forbes; Trevor Fray; Patricia Frith; Lynn Goold; Maureen Gough; Kenneth Greenwood; Steven Greenwood; Susan Hanson; Tom Hargreaves; Christine Holliday; Irene Holloway; Mr N. Honeybone; Betty Hooper; Philip J. Howard; Lynn Hudson; Pat Hursey; Jacky James; Barbara Jefford; Margaret Jenkinson; Mavis Johns; Mrs. B. Jackson; Terry Ladlow; Joy Lewis; Griff Loydd; Lewis Lumb; Beryl

Marston; S. McConnell; Barbara Miller; Pamela Moll; Edward Motteram; Jean Parsons; Joe Pearce; Isabel Pickering; Richard Pope; Eric Portman (cousin); Ian Portman; John Portman; Michael Portman; Frank Ravlen; Tim Raymond; S. W. Robertshaw; John R. Rowthorn; Gwen Rudman; June Salt Becky Sharpe; Kenneth Shilling; Alan Sidney-Wilmot; Professor Andrew Spicer; Frank Stanford; Paul Tritton; Doris Vincent; Donald Walker; Jane Walter; Paul Weatherhogg; Roger Whear; Ann Whittington; Anne Womersley (nee Portman).

Thanks as always for invaluable help to the highly recommended *The Writers' and Artists' Yearbook* (A & C Black) available in all good bookshops and a must for all writers.

A big thank you also to Bryan Forbes, CBE, and the late Richard Briers, CBE, who replied to my letters for information about their time working with Eric Portman.

And finally, thanks to Jane and Nigel Evans of Sigma Press for commissioning the book proposal after several publishers and literary agents turned it down.

SELECTIVE INDEX

A
A Call on Kuprin: Part One, 178
A Canterbury Tale, 80
A Double Life, 169-171
A Hundred Years Old, 52
A Night at the Hardcastles, 52
A Tale of Two Cities, 171
A Touch of the Poet, 171-174
Abdul the Damned, 43
Anderson, Michael, 178
The Aristocrats, 23-24
Assignment To Kill, 187

B
Basten, Jill, 117
Banbury, Frith, 175-176
Barraclough, Mildred, 166
Baynton, Henry, 27, 29, 30
The Blind Goddess, 109, 118
Bitter Harvest, 45, 50
The Blind Goddess, 110-112
Bolt, Robert, 175-176
Bottomley, C.E.D., 23, 194
Breheny, Betty, 124
Brill, Cazz, 185-186
Broadfield, Joyce, 192-193
Briers, CBE, Richard, 7, 187
Broom, Christine, 93
The Browning Version, 113-118

C
Caine, Michael, 186-187
Cairo Road, 90, 123
The Cardinal, 43
Chase The Ace, 40
Child in the House, 167
Chu Chin Chow, 41-42
Connolly, J.W, 87

Corridor of Mirrors, 103-109
Crawshaw, Daphne, 90
The Crimes of Stephen Hawke, 44

D
Danton, 48
Darlow, Michael, 114-115
Daybreak, 85, 112
Deadfall, 186-187
Dear Murderer 35, 86
Desert Island Discs, 136
Dewhirst, Cyril, 23
Dewhirst, Morris, 23
Diplomacy, 40,

E
Earnshaw, Tony, 7, 109, 169, 178, 183
Escape to Danger, 79
Evans, Dame Edith, 186

F
Ferguson, Barbara, 94
Ferguson, John, 90-94
Ferguson, Mike, 90
Field, Shirley Anne, 169-170
Flowering Cherry, 175-176
Forbes, CBE, Bryan, 186-187
Forbes, Mr F., 174
Flynn, Errol, 48-49
The 49th Parallel, 55-69
Freud: The Secret Passion, 179-180

G
Gee, Nellie 23
The Girl of Maxim's, 41
Give Me Yesterday, 51
Glover, David, 18, 192
The Golden Mask, 130

Great Day, 81
The Great Romancer, 50
The Guilty Party, 126, 131

H
Halifax Civic Trust, 18
Harlequinade, 114-115
Harrison, Alice - see Portman, Alice (mother)
Hearts of Humanity, 43
Hiller, Dame Wendy, 175-176
His Excellency (play), 123-125
His Excellency (film), 128-129
Holliday, Christine, 88
Holloway, Irene, 116-117, 124-125, 173, 183, 191-192
Holroyd, Sybil, 40
Hooper, Betty, 117
Hyde Park Corner, 42
Hudson, Lynn, 118
Hursey, Pat, 119

I
I Have Been Here Before, 51
The Intruder, 51, 53
The Importance of Being Earnest, 39-40

J
Jackson, Mrs B., 87-88
Jeannie, 51
Jenkinson, Margaret, 23
Julius Caesar, 50
Johns, Mavis, 93
Justice, 188-189

L
Ladlow, Terry, 190-191
Laing, Knox, 89-98, 192
Lee Christopher, 109
The Living Room, 135

Loyd, Griff, 137-138

M
Macaulay, Pauline 183
Madam Bouvary, 51, 69
The Magic Box, 126
Maria Marten, or Murder in the Red Barn, 42
The Mark of Cain, 87
Marston, Beryl, 118
Mask of Kings, 51
Medawar, Margaret, 22, 168-169
Men of Two Worlds, 81-82
Midsummer Fires, 40
Millions Like Us, 77-78
Moll, Pamela, 120
The Moment of Truth, 136
Monroe, Marilyn, 170
Moonlight Sonata, 45
Moorcroft, Eric, 20-21, 25, 27
Motteram, Edward, 69, 125
Mr Betts Runs Away, 167
Mrs Siddons, 40-41
Murray, Barbara, 188

N
Naked Edge, 177-178
Newth, Jontathan, 183-184

O
On The Spot, 3
One Of Our Aircraft is Missing, 69
Old Roses, 42
Oliver Twist, 174

P
Pickles, Wilfred, 25, 30-31, 194
Perdita - see *Harlequinade*
The Pelicans, 52
Playbill, 113-117
Pleasure Island, 135

The Poison Road, 127
Portman, Ada, 134,
Portman, Albert, 133
Portman, Alice (nee Harrison) (Eric's mother), 18, 22
Portman, Alice, (Eric's sister-in-law), 59, 119, 122
Portman, Charles Clifford (Cliff), 19-20, 27, 120
Portman, Eric (namesake), 133-135
Portman, Ernest, 21
Portman, Eva, 134
Portman, Frank Leslie (Leslie), 19-20, 26-27, 59, 119, 122
Portman, Friend, 131
Portman, Ian, 21
Portman, Harold, 131
Portman, James, 19
Portman, John, 27
Portman, John Edward, 131, 133
Portman, Sarah Jane, 131
Portman, Winifred May, (Winnie), 19, 27, 12
Portman and Pickles (pub, Halifax), 193
Powell, Michael, 55-71
Pressburger, Emeric, 55-71
Priestley, J. B., 51
The Prince and the Pauper, 48-49

R
Rattigan, Terence, 89, 113-117, 145-147
Raymond, Tim, 96
The Rivals, 40
Robertshaw, Shirley, 24,25
Robson, Floa, 35-36
Romney, Edana, 105-109

S
Separate Tables, 145-166, 167, 169-171

Sidney-Wilmot, Alan, 35, 68-69
Sidney-Wilmot, R. C., 68
The Singing Marine, 49
Slaughter, Tod, 42, 44
South of Algiers, 130
The Spider and the Fly, 120
Satterfit, Harriet, 19
Squadron Leader X, 74-75

T
Table By The Window, 145-167
Table Number Seven, 145-167
This Desirable Residence, 43
Thunder Rock, 69

U
Uncensored, 71-72
Uncle Harry, 71-73, 79

V
Vincent, Doris, 92-93

W
Walker, Donald, 147, 154-166
Wanted for Murder, 84, 118
Warner Brothers, 48
We Dive at Dawn, 76-77
West 11, 180
Whear, Roger, 185
Whetter, Emily, 94
Whetter, Henry, 94
Whetter, Mabel, 93-94
White Cargo, 35
The World of Light, 40

Z
Zero Hour, 82

* Index supplied by the author